OUR FATHER'S LOVE

OUR FATHER'S LOVE

DISCOVERING JESUS IN THE ABSENCE OF MY DAD

BRENTON A. HOLBROOK

HOLY WATER
PRESS

ISBN: 979-8-9987537-0-1
Published by: Holy Water Press, LLC. Mount Pleasant, MI

Library of Congress Control Number: 2025909778

First Edition, 2025

Printed in the United States of America

Disclaimer:
This book contains the author's personal experiences and reflections. It is not intended as professional counseling or therapy. Readers are strongly encouraged to seek counseling and/or therapy from a licensed mental health professional.

For information about author appearances or other general inquiries, please contact:

info@holywaterpress.com

Typesetting services by BOOKOW.COM

DEDICATION

To Our Father, who demonstrated His love for us by sacrificing His Son on the Cross so that we may genuinely experience His abounding love and mercy.

To my hero, my mother, Penny.
My encourager, my protector, the one who was instrumental in helping me to find Jesus, and who ferociously protected me and loved me deeply in those difficult years.
Rest In Peace, Mom.
(1960-2022)

To my sister and brother, Tiffany and Joshua, for making their own marks on my life during those difficult years and being the best siblings I could ever have.

To all the fathers out there who sacrifice every day for the betterment of their children.

And finally, to my father, Volley, who inspired this book, and for his triumphs, accomplishments, and sacrifices in becoming the father he is today.
I love you, Dad.

PREFACE

We all have a story, a journey that is uniquely ours, one that is shaped by the experiences that we've endured, by the people we've encountered, and by the paths that we've chosen to walk. My story begins with a tragedy, one that leaves the deepest of voids in the hearts of men and women, young boys and girls around the World; The absence of a father.

The deep and unshakable desire for a father's love is something that is indescribable. Whether your situation echoes mine, or even if death separated you from your father, it doesn't matter. The void and darkness can still be there, and if you have experienced this heartbreak, I welcome you here. I pray that the Lord shines His light to guide you through this darkness, just as He did for me, and I hope that He chooses to use this book as His tool in helping you.

Growing up without my dad was not just a fact of life; it was a profound emptiness that influenced every aspect of my being. An emptiness that I still struggle to articulate adequately even today. I searched for that missing piece in different places and with different people, trying to understand who I was and where I belonged. For a long while, the absence of my father left me feeling incomplete, unworthy, and lost.

On the contrary to what you may have expected, this book is not about the absence; it's about what I found in that void. It is about a discovery like none other. A discovery of a love so powerful and bountiful that it filled the deepest chasms in my heart. This is the story of how I met Jesus Christ, the one who becomes a Father to the fatherless. He showed me a love beyond measure and filled that chasm that separated me from a life of purpose and peace, and He is the one who lead me to the same.

Within these pages I've written letters to my younger self, offering the wisdom and comfort I wish I had known then. These letters reflect the journey I've traveled- from the pain of abandonment to the joy of spiritual discovery. They are a testament to the transformative power of God's love and a reminder that we are never truly alone.

Whether you have experienced fatherlessness, are searching for meaning, or are seeking to deepen your faith, I hope my story resonates with you. This entire book is my prayer that you are inspired to look beyond your circumstances and find the unshakable, unwavering love of our Heavenly Father.

Thank you so much for joining me on this journey. I hope and pray that you find comfort, peace, and healing within these pages and I'll meet with you again at the end to see how far you've come, so let's get started.

Your Brother in Christ,
Brenton

ACKNOWLEDGMENTS

Many thanks are extended to Tammy A. and Judy C. for serving as my beta readers and providing the initial set of edits and constructive criticism.

They enabled me to hone in on what my tone would be, and I hope I kept to it.

ACKNOWLEDGMENTS

CONTENTS

Chapter 1

THE VOID

Hᴇʏ Bubba,

I know it's weird to read your nickname to yourself, but I had to get your attention. I'm you but from the future. I know it's funny, and you won't believe this, but that's okay. As you read these letters, I think you will begin to understand what is happening. I am using these letters to give you the advice that I know you are yearning for right now, even if you can't verbalize what you are searching for.

I see you. You have so much confusion and pain in your heart, and you don't know what to do with it. The questions swirling around right now will linger for years to come, slowly filtering out as you learn and grow, shaping who you are and how you see yourself. You will wonder where your place is and how you can impact others the most. I know that despite all this pain you're experiencing, you want to help others so they don't have to feel what you've felt or to the degree you've felt it. This shadow clouding the light from around you causes you to question your situation. A pervasive feeling that something is missing, or rather someone.

That shadow is where your father should be. Unfortunately, that shadow will stretch far into your life. It will affect you profoundly despite those days that seem ordinary. You will play outside with other kids, laughing and having fun, but that shadow darkens your life on different days. These days come and go but are random. They are the little things you've noticed along the way like Mike's dad coming to pick him up from school, while yours didn't. That's when the questions started. Where is my dad? Why isn't he picking me up from school like the other kids?

Since I'm you, I know what you haven't said out loud. You never fully voiced these questions and the feelings underneath them, did you? Perhaps it was because you were scared or couldn't speak to the heartache. The answers that potentially awaited you surely could hurt you, and that was the last thing you wanted added to your plate. Instead of being outspoken, you buried these questions and feelings, hoping they would disappear. They didn't, of course. The hurt and heartache grew uncontrollably, becoming part of who you were, the little boy without a dad, trying to figure out where he belonged. When the pressure was too much, Mom would answer some of the questions on your mind. Still, she only gave the minimum amount of information until you were old enough to understand the situation.

I remember the day your teacher asked everyone to draw a picture of their family. It was a quiet afternoon, one of those ordinary days, at least until now. How could you draw something you didn't understand? Your definition of family wasn't like the other kids in class. With Bill as your stepdad, you still don't feel he belongs on the page where your dad should be. I remember the decision to draw four stick figures and a house. Mom, Tiffany, Joshua, and you, no dad on the other side of the page, just blank space. That was how it felt, too. You just felt empty inside. You were a puzzle missing its last piece, always looking for something you couldn't find. It's crazy how something as simple as a hand-drawn picture can say so much.

This emptiness you were feeling only became more pronounced as you got older. It was just the small things at first, like when Grandpa had to teach you how to tie a tie because nobody else could. Eventually, the more significant things made it all worse. When you fell hard for Kayla, your first crush, or Amber, your first kiss, you had nobody to talk to about how you felt when it eventually went awry. When you grow up to be the man writing you this letter, you reflect on those moments and remember them fondly. Still, some good news is that it doesn't change the man you become despite being unable to talk to anybody about them. Several people in your life tried to help you along, like Mom, for instance. She did her best and was a superhero in her own right, but she couldn't possibly fill the voids God never intended for her to fill. That role was entrusted to Dad, but something else got in his way, as life often does, whether we want it to or not. Regardless, a child needs their father, even if they don't understand at the time.

You became adept at hiding your emotions. An unfortunate power of many around the world, you were able to hide how you truly felt. You were able to hold back your tears and pain. The only sign you were hurting was a subtle crack in your voice after you suppressed the initial emotion. Many people refer to this as wearing a mask. You wore this mask anytime it came up in conversation. You pretended it didn't bother you that Dad wasn't around despite the hurt you were experiencing. The absence of your father was a wound that never healed, always lingering below the surface, influencing your life choices and shaping your identity in ways you can't yet comprehend. So, you searched. You sought out a father elsewhere, hoping to fill the void.

You looked to almost any adult, teachers, and even your friends' fathers, seeking the approval and guidance you craved. But more was always needed because nobody could fill the role that your father left vacant. There were nights when you would lie awake, staring at the ceiling, wondering why he wasn't there. You tried piecing together fragments of stories you heard from friends and family, only to find that they never added to the entire story. The questions swirled around in your mind, relentless and unanswered. Why did he leave? Why hasn't he come back to me? Do I have anything to do with it? Was it something I did?

These questions become part of you. They will shape your self-worth and understanding of love. You begin to believe that maybe love was something you had to earn, something that could be taken away if you weren't careful. You become anxious and cautious about the most minuscule issues, guarding your heart against the possibility of more pain and abandonment. You quickly realize that this only grew loneliness, didn't it?

You heard that, didn't you? The whisper in your heart. You've listened to it several times but didn't know what to think. A faint glimmer of hope amid all this pain and sorrow. You did not know it then, but this was where you began your journey to discovering a different kind of Father. A Father who would never leave you. A Father whose love was constant and unchanging. A Father who would leave the ninety-nine to come and find you. What an exhilarating feeling, but that cannot be true. That is not what that whisper was, was it?

Brenton, this is where our story begins. It begins with a boy who feels lost, abandoned, and incomplete, and ends with a man who discovers a profound love that changes everything. This journey is lengthy and full of twists and turns, but it all begins with a simple letter to the boy I once was.

You don't know this yet, but a Father has been watching over you all these years. He was there in the quiet moments when the hot, silent tears streamed down your face, relieving the pressure of the pain built up inside your heart. He was there on those sleepless nights when you were afraid to be alone in the dark. When no one else was watching over you as you slept, He was. Guarding you all night long with legions of His angels following His every command and ready to shield you from harm. He loves you. He protects you. He was waiting for you to grow and learn of Him. He was waiting for you to realize that you were never truly alone. He was waiting for you to come home.

Hold on, Brenton. Your story is just beginning.

When I speak of the void, I talk of nagging emptiness in your heart and soul. It's a cave you yell into, only to hear echoes in return. The problem, though, is that those echoes are my anxieties and depression, striking me from all angles, seemingly out of nowhere. Whenever it comes up in conversation, I often feel zoned out. In my mind, I'm in a crowded room with strangers looking at me, knowing I'm that kid without his dad. I am that awkward kid who never learned to socialize and interact with peers the "normal" way and the one who was always weird to talk to. Empty, broken, alone, confused, and lost are the main feelings around this part of my life, and they spill over into my life as an adult. These feelings describe how I felt through high school. I experienced no validation from a paternal source, so I felt that nothing I did would ever measure up. I often thought that I didn't deserve friends because I would inevitably let them down, so I kept to myself for the most part. I spoke to others only when necessary because I felt that it was inevitable that I would do something or say something to embarrass myself.

As rational adults with mature, developed, and experienced minds, we know this could not be further from the truth. The situation handed to me was not my doing nor my fault, and it was not even close. In my specific case, the problem resulted from the personal choices of my father, choosing a vice over his son. However, the thoughts and memories in these early chapters of my life are immature thoughts of a child who has no idea why the world works the way it does. While it may seem dramatic, the thoughts are an outlier on the far end of the spectrum; these are the logical, natural thoughts of a young boy who doesn't understand life yet. The questions I speak of are usually the first ones that come to my mind: "Is it my fault?" "Did I do something wrong?" "Does my dad not love me?"

Before I continue further, I'll slide in a quick disclaimer. Throughout this book, I can only repeat what I remember and the reality it created. The adage of perception is reality comes into play here. In addition, some pieces of what I've heard in stories recounted to me from others are also present. By piecing together these stories, my mind has created an illusion of memory that may not have happened or happened in a way different from how I perceived it while I was young. This makes my story extraordinarily difficult to tell because the earlier the "memories," the harder it is to recount them as accurately as possible. I will articulate it as clearly as I can… When I attempt to recall specific memories, I will not say everything on the following pages is exactly how it happened. Still, it is how I *perceived* it to happen. Unfortunately, that is enough because your mind plays tricks on you. Your mind is more potent than most give it credit for, so forgive me if some details need to be more accurate.

The earliest memories are simply flashbacks. In my mind, I recall a few moments with Dad, much like a Hollywood montage. It was before he left, but I remember the first moment at a park pavilion. We must have been having a party or attending a family reunion. Still, I remember my father being there, joking with everyone and flexing his muscles in the rain. That day it rained heavily, and he was completely soaked. At some point after that, I remember going to see him. He had moved into his apartment at this point, and I don't recall even wondering why he did so. I remember eating graham crackers with some milk and sugar on top. A treat I still eat from time to time, even now, well into adulthood. But the next thing I remember about that day is my mom frantically picking me up. If I recall correctly, Mom told me a while later, when I was older, that someone called the paramedics after finding me running up and down the balcony of the apartment complex. They grabbed me and traced me back to Dad's apartment, seeing that he had passed out in the other room. And that was it. That was the last memory I had of him. Passed out. I thought he was taking a nap.

My older sister Tiffany, my older brother Joshua, and I all lived with Mom in a small apartment on the north side of Grand Rapids. We lived in Apartment 202. Please don't ask me how I remember that because I recall so many random things from this point in my life. Still, they've never made sense and seem insignificant, so I've never considered it much. I remember hearing plenty of stories about this phase of our lives. Mom worked at the apartment complex as a maintenance staff member, and her friend was the lady in the leasing office. Mom also worked as the lifeguard at the pool, a job I decided to test one day, causing a lady to scream that there was a baby at the bottom of the deep end. Mom sure was surprised to learn that it was me! As I write this sentence, I recall that my dad may have had something to do with this, too… For some reason, I remember Mom telling me once that he fell asleep while watching me. I wandered over to the pool and got into the situation I described. Either way, I was in the pool and tested Mom's lifeguarding skills. They were pretty good, considering I'm here to tell this story, and she used to volunteer for the American Red Cross emergency response unit.

Shortly after that memory, my mind is blank, most likely due to my young age. That is, until a new man started coming around. His name was Bill. He was nice to me and was another person who saved my life. I was playing a board game by myself and started to choke. I couldn't breathe, and I went to my mom and Bill. I was probably four years old then, and I remember him giving me the Heimlich maneuver. Out of my mouth came a green raindrop-shaped game piece from the board game. Maybe I should change my middle name to "Danger." After Bill started coming around, I realized something was missing. I knew that Bill wasn't my dad, but I realized that my dad wasn't around because of that knowledge. Bill was a good man; he had his faults, but in the end, we all do. I firmly believe that God placed Bill in my life despite his faults. After all, he stepped up and cared for a little boy who needed someone, making him one of the primary father figures in my life. (I discuss father figures more in-depth in a later chapter.)

I noticed that after Bill married my mother, he started showing up at school events. He would contribute financially to classroom parties, school carnivals, choir concerts, book fairs, and take-home fundraisers, as well as assist me in soliciting donations from our neighbors. I give him that credit because it allowed us to make wonderful memories together. In the end, it is difficult to say he was not the man I needed in my life. Once I began to make these mental connections, one of the first memories I have of my dad not being there was when I had to wait in line for the school bus outside my classroom. As I patiently waited for Bus #110 to turn the corner, I watched as kid after kid was escorted out of school by their moms and dads, and I remember feeling envious. I was sad and angry that I didn't have something as simple as that to experience. The emotions I felt lit a fire in my belly that I couldn't quench. That's not to say that Bill or Mom never came to pick me up on occasion. It means that the simplest things can mean the most, and sometimes they can mean everything. And when that "thing," whatever it may be for you, isn't satisfied, it hurts on the deepest levels. I was so confused at this point that there was a time that I didn't go by my legal surname of Holbrook; I went by Bill's surname and the name Mom took when she married him. Looking back, this was the first symptom of my later issues with identity. The way I saw it, why should I carry the name of a man who wasn't around?

On the deepest level, for me, abandonment and being forgotten were the worst. The entire paternal side of my family seemed like they had forgotten about my existence. In absolute truth, I hold them accountable for that because nobody else came to visit me except for my half-sisters Melinda and Tarina. When they visited, it was to say hello and give Mom the latest updates on Dad. Even then, it only happened a few times. The update was typical: where he was most recently, what he was doing, and the trouble he was getting into. Even my grandfather didn't visit me, and that hurts because I've heard nothing but good stories about him and how he was a good man. A man who was never afraid to get his hands dirty or work hard and earn something. My grandfather is someone I brag about despite never meeting him as I got older. His accomplishments and the work he involved himself in were impressive. During World War II, he joined the US Navy as a Gunner's Mate and survived two ship sinkings. After the war, he came home to Michigan. He was an ironworker by the late 50s, with the Mackinac Bridge being the highest-profile project he participated in. At just under five miles long, it was once the longest suspension bridge in the world, spanning the Straits of Mackinac and connecting the Upper and Lower Peninsulas of Michigan. Other than that, I, to this day, have minimal information and relationships with the paternal side of my family.

Just when I thought my situation couldn't get any worse, the most difficult feelings of abandonment struck the day my dad called Mom. I was probably six or seven then, and he told her he was in town and wanted to see us. Mom recalled this story to me years later, but I remember her saying that a lot of convincing occurred because she didn't trust him. Still, eventually, she decided it was best for me to see him at least, so they made plans for him to come over. I remember Mom telling me that her biggest regret about this story was telling me that he had called her and the plans they made. I remember sitting in the living room in Bill's recliner, waiting for my dad to show up. I watched television quietly but happily as I waited. I waited quite a while until I got tired and decided to take a nap, so I made a little sign that said to wake me up as soon as Dad arrived, and I fell asleep, but he never showed up. A few hours later, I woke up in bed, and it was already dark outside. I knew at that moment what had transpired, and I began to cry.

I remember crying while Mom was holding me. I don't know what happened in our conversation, but I remember how that anger and hatred began to build up again. That was the second time I felt that fire in my belly. It was hot and intense. It was such a foreign feeling to me, so against my general nature. Growing up in that house was primarily happy, at least for me. So, the feeling I was experiencing was a complete one-eighty. It honestly made me sick to my stomach that first time. Over time, these feelings would revisit me. Still, eventually, I had to either deal with them appropriately or go down a destructive path. Thankfully, other plans would prosper me, not harm me, and give me hope and a future. I am so thankful that those plans were already in place and working because life could have turned out so much differently had I gone down the destructive path like so many other kids in the world without a father.

After Dad didn't visit me that day, I never heard from him again until I was about eleven, and I began a heavy push to find others who would fill in for him. Unfortunately, this was another area where I experienced the feeling of abandonment. I understand why now that I'm an adult. It is an awkward area to be put in as an adult; your heart is pulling you one way because you understand the child's situation, but your mind is pulling you elsewhere because you are not the child's father. It is the responsibility of the custodial parent to handle this issue. It's unfortunate to experience, but these days, the saying "it takes a village" sometimes rings true and sometimes doesn't apply.

For me, John Alanowski was a father figure. John was the father of my best friend, Mike. Mike and I met in kindergarten in Mrs. B's class. We hit it off as friends and quickly learned we only lived a block away from each other's houses. So began the play dates, pool parties, and a friendship filled with craziness and shenanigans. When I looked at John and Mike's relationship, I was left with some bittersweet feelings. I felt the same feelings as before: Envy, Sadness, and Anger. I also felt happy for Mike because he had what I hadn't experienced. John was the strong, albeit stubborn, man that Mike needed. Mike was born with cerebral palsy, and his childhood was not easy. With one side of his body slightly weaker and less capable, he had to learn to do everything other kids did, including what we take for granted, such as walking. It was always more of a challenge for him because he had to figure out how to complete tasks in ways he was physically capable of. Operating a commercial lawn mower and driving a pickup truck are great examples of this, and the fact that Mike can still kick my butt playing Call of Duty, but let's not go there, though.

I briefly alluded earlier to the fact that the absence of a father in life, especially in the formative years of childhood, can leave lasting damage to the psyche of a person. As they grow older, they will likely be able to sort out some of those aches and pains, but not all of them. For me, I find that I still struggle deeply with unaddressed anguish, like self-sabotage, for example. In many settings, personal and professional, I begin to doubt my abilities at the slightest mistake. I would get written up at work for a minuscule issue, but my mind would compound that issue and lead to others. Eventually, my anxiety and depression would take over, leaving me nearly useless and unable to function. Finally, I would usually terminate the relationship or my employment on my own before I had to explain myself or if I felt I would be fired. It was a destructive, self-coping, self-protective mechanism. I didn't want to discuss why I am the way I am. I didn't want to reveal how broken I was. The internal thought that I can never measure up to anything or be a productive member of society is difficult to process. These symptoms or self-coping mechanisms may vary for each person struggling with fatherlessness. Still, they all come from the father's wound, at least to some degree.

I'm not a mental health professional, so I don't have any insight into these feelings or where they come from. But I can tell you how I made my way out. It was significant support from my loved ones, the friends

I trusted with this story, and the One the book is about. I first sought mental health assistance from the Department of Veterans Affairs in 2015, and my experience was less than satisfactory. I started shopping around Grand Rapids and eventually found Jason. I met Jason in 2017 or 2018 through a search on psychologytoday.com. He was listed on the website as having worked with military and public safety personnel.

I made an appointment and gave it a try. It wasn't one specific appointment, but throughout many sessions, Jason helped to break the spiderweb of mental health. The emotions, the bad memories, the trauma, and the idea that I wasn't worth anything. Jason was the one who did the initial work on the impact fatherlessness had on me. He was the one who laid a layer of strength to the foundation that I was trying to build inside myself. He helped me to see that healing was possible. Recovery from mental illness was possible, even in the most traumatic experiences. I want to acknowledge what happened and what caused me to experience and seek that healing. To this day, I recommend everyone to see a therapist, even if you feel like there isn't much going on. Sometimes, getting some things off your chest is good, and you will thank yourself later.

Chapter 2

THE SEARCH FOR IDENTITY

D EAR Me,
This was the moment that changed everything. Still young, but carrying the heaviest of questions and hurt never meant for your age, but nonetheless, it had become so familiar to you. You needed a compass and needed to know where to turn. You couldn't find the love you so desperately needed, but at this moment, everything was about to change. This wasn't a Hollywood screenplay, so there weren't loud claps of thunder and booming voices from the heavens. It was much quieter and gentler than that, and it came from inside you, deep-seated in your chest and heart. It was the same whisper you'd heard before so many times, but this time was different. It was an invitation. An invitation that felt as if it came from someone you knew and trusted.

Mom and Bill took you to a new church that morning, choosing to sit toward the back few rows. This morning, we were visiting a church that didn't own its own building yet, so they rented space from Rockford Public Schools on Sundays. Here we sat in the cafeteria, turned sanctuary. Hesitant and shy initially, you didn't know what to say or how to feel. You weren't used to church yet; it wasn't something we did often. It wasn't until recently that we began "shopping" for a new place to go. Until then, we were basically holiday attendees, only going on major holidays like Christmas or Easter.

Then the music began. You'd heard the songs before with Mom, but this time was different. There was something special about how the band sang and blended their voices. The lyrics they sang addressed a part of you that had been dark and silent for far too long. The lyrics were simple, but they touched your heart in a way you couldn't explain. Something you could feel but not see told you that this was the right place for you right now. There was some confusion on your part because the church felt like a place for people who already had their lives together. It was for people who didn't struggle with the weight that you felt at such an early age.

Eventually, the kids were invited to the children's church when the songs ended. Mom and Bill encouraged you to go, so you wandered along with the other kids. The Sunday school teacher spoke of a Father in Heaven, a God who loved His children unconditionally and would never abandon them. She talked about Jesus, a Savior who came to Earth willingly to die in our place so that we could experience God's unlimited love in a deeply profound way. A love so powerful that it could make the sad things seem small. That wonderful lady said that all you had to do to experience that love is to ask God into your heart and that He would love you in ways you never felt before.

So, when the kids bowed their heads to pray, that was precisely what you did. You asked God to be your Father, just as the lady said that God was her Father, too. Your words washed over you like a gentle spring breeze, and you felt something inside your heart for the first time. Could it be true? Could there be a Father who loved you as immensely as that lady said? A Father that wouldn't leave you like your biological Father did? Could there be a love that didn't depend on your performance, on whether you were good enough, smart enough, or worthy enough? You didn't magically receive all the answers you were seeking, but at that moment, you felt something you hadn't felt in a long time. Peace. It wasn't the peace that came from understanding everything or answering all the questions you had swirling around in your mind. The peace came from knowing now and acknowledging that you weren't alone in this world. There was a God who saw you, knew your pain, and wanted to fill the void in your heart.

When the children's church was over, you were sent back into the main room with Mom and Bill. They were just wrapping everything up and were about to dismiss when the Pastor gave an altar call for anyone wanting to come forward for prayer. You felt that same nudge in your chest that you had felt only moments ago. This time, it was telling you that it was time to move. The next thing you knew, you were halfway to the front of the room in the center aisle. It felt like your legs had been taken over, and you were a robot without control. You looked up and received prayer from a prayer team member in front of the room, and it was a fantastic feeling.

It was on this day that something inside you changed. It was like a door had been opened in your heart, allowing a sliver of light to enter the darkness surrounding you for so long. You didn't know it then, but this was the beginning of your faith journey, leading you to discover a love greater than anything you had ever known. As you walked out of church that day with Mom and Bill, you felt lighter, a burden lifted from your shoulders. The world seemed a little brighter, a little more hopeful. You didn't fully understand what happened, but you knew something had shifted. For the first time, you felt the stirrings of faith. The beginning of a relationship with the God who would become the Father you needed the most.

At this point, I wish that I could tell you everything was simple from then on. But faith isn't a magic cure-all for life's problems. It is a journey often filled with challenges, doubts, setbacks, and moments that require deep trust in the Lord. At the same time, it is a journey filled with grace, love, and the steady, reassuring presence of a God who never leaves His children. This first encounter of faith was just the beginning. It was the seed that would grow, slowly but surely, into a deep, abiding relationship with God. You couldn't see the whole picture back then, but from my perspective, that moment was the turning point. A moment when you began to see that there was hope, love, and a Father to be had. One who had been waiting for you all along.

So, hold onto this memory, Brenton. Always remember the day in that gymnasium turned Sunday school, where you sat on the free-throw line of the basketball court and asked God into your heart. Remember that school cafeteria turned sanctuary where you went up for prayer. Turn this memory into your foundation. The foundation that will support you as you become the man writing you this letter and lock it away in your mind. This was the day that faith first took root in your heart. This faith is what will carry you through the years to come. It will be your anchor, guide, and most significant source of strength. And know this: the same God who met you in church that day is with you even now, guiding you, loving you, and holding you close.

You are never alone.

Who am I?

This question has echoed around in my head for years. I'm sure it has echoed around the hearts and minds of many people over the years, and for those of us who grew up without a father, it can feel like a haunting refrain. Without the guidance and affirmation a father is meant to provide, the search for identity becomes a journey riddled with confusion, doubt, and false starts. We look to our surroundings to find something to anchor to. Our friends, achievements, relationships, anything to tell us who we are.

What I've realized is that the external markers of identity often fall short. They are subject to change. They shift and fade away, leaving us feeling even more lost than before. Listen to me intently here and pay attention to the pronoun that I have used. You need to find *who* can define you. The answer is a person, not a thing. Ladies, your identity is not in your body, your physical beauty, or anything of vanity. Guys, your identity is not in your ability to fly under the radar, providing for your family single-handedly without complaint or attention to your needs. Men often sacrifice their mental health and hide their pain from their families so they can provide materially.

We often wonder who will provide us with the answer to the identity question. Well, I'll give you the answer: Jesus Christ. Only by turning to the One who created and saved us can we begin to discover and uncover the truth about ourselves. People all over the world often wonder what our purpose is on Earth and what we are meant to do here. Well, our life's purpose is to give praise and glory to the One who created us. We are commanded to honor, respect, and love Him with our hearts, minds, and souls.

Often, it gets confused that purpose is what we are supposed to do professionally, and that isn't it at all. The Holy Spirit gives each of us gifts to bless and love on others. This is so that by performing our professions, we are able to bless others with our labor. It is not to slap a label on our bodies like a nametag and say: "This is my purpose! This is who I'm meant to be!" It is by loving and believing in God that we are able to find the purpose meant for us. To ask Him to bless our labor so that, in so doing, we offer it to Him and His purposes.

Growing up without a father leaves a void that is hard to describe. Fathers are meant to be mirrors, reflecting back to their children a sense of worth, capability, and belonging. In all three of those departments, I have struggled significantly. I struggle, especially in the areas of capability and belonging. I humorously describe myself as a recovering introvert. All through school, I was usually shy. In the rare times that I wasn't, I was socially awkward. I didn't really have many friends, but I also didn't have enemies either. I was kind of a loner, out on my own. My sense of belonging because of this was distorted.

Capability is one that I now struggle with as an adult. As a first-time homebuyer, I ended up buying a nice home, but it was one that needed work. I didn't know this at the time, as the surface level looked great to me and the inspector, but as always, the things lurking underneath only came out after living in the home. Some electrical work needs to be done, some general repairs, and major replacements to the furnace and windows all need to happen. My problem is that I want to be the stereotypical dad who knows how to do all these things, but I don't because nobody taught me. It leaves me feeling both worthless and helpless, always begging for someone else to bail me out of a project. It always seems like when I start something on my own, it always goes awry.

So, when your father is not present, and the mirror reflects only yourself, what do you do? It's easy to feel like we're staring into darkness, trying to piece together who we are from these fragmented glimpses of ourselves. And for me, this void showed up early. I remember feeling much different from my peers, who seemed to be confident and seemed to have a sense of who they were. They spoke of family traditions and fatherly advice while I quietly wrestled with questions that I mostly had no idea how to articulate. How do I ask such questions when I don't have words for them? Am I enough? Am I loved? Do I matter? Without a father answering these questions, I turned to the world around me for validation.

When you don't know who you are, it is tempting to let others influence your self-perception. As a teenager, I tried building my identity on achievements. If I got good grades (which I didn't, by the way), maybe I'd be seen as smart. If I excelled in sports (which I didn't), maybe I would be considered valuable. These are just examples, but I wore accomplishments like masks. I hoped that they would convince others that I was worth something. Unfortunately, external validation is a fickle foundation. No matter what kind or how much praise I received, it was never enough. The void in my heart was like the Grand Canyon, so good luck filling that up, Brenton. If I failed, even slightly, it felt like my entire identity crumbled. A perfect example for me in school was mathematics. In school, I never grasped math. I only passed with D's. It wasn't until I was an adult that basic skills began to make sense to me. Eventually, I began to realize that basing my self-worth on what I could do was exhausting and unsustainable. But where else was I supposed to go?

My turning point came when I asked Jesus Christ into my heart on that cold gymnasium floor while sitting on the free throw line. Once I encountered faith for the first time, I began to see myself through a different lens. Not through the lens of my accomplishments, my failures, or the opinions of others, but through the lens of God's inexhaustible love. The Bible speaks of a God who called me His child, who formed me in my mother's womb, and who loves me unconditionally. This truth was both comforting and disorienting. How could I matter so much to a God who I barely knew?

But the more I leaned into my faith in Him, the more I began to understand that my identity is in Him. It's in Him. It wasn't something that I had to earn. It was something I already had the entire time. God had created me with purpose and value, and no amount of success or failure could ever change what God had done. It was written in my heart, yet I never knew. As I began to learn how to see myself as God sees me, it replaced the old fickle foundation with one where I was standing on solid rock. It was the foundation of a new understanding of my self-worth. It felt so good to have my feet on solid ground.

I want to revisit my discussion on the difference between identity and purpose for a moment. The distinction between these two is perhaps one of the most transformative lessons I've ever learned. I conflated them for a long time, believing that what I did translated somehow into who I was. Identity is about being, whereas purpose is about doing. Earlier, I mentioned that the Holy Spirit gives each of us gifts to use. This is what I meant. By understanding that we are God's children, we are called to do unto others as we would have them do unto us. It is clear to me now that because I am a child of God, I am called to be His light unto the world. To show care, love, compassion, and mercy to everyone through the work we do.

My identity is firmly rooted in the unchanging fact that I am a child of God, loved and chosen by Him. My purpose, on the other hand, is how I am supposed to live out my identity in the world. It is the unique calling that God has given me and placed into my life. It is shaped by my gifts, passions, and experiences. Understanding this distinction was crucial in finally feeling free. It meant that I could face setbacks in my purpose without questioning my worth because my identity remained secure. Nothing can pluck me from the Father's hand. My place is secure, but it does come with the expectation that I remain loyal to Him and that I obey His word.

Even after I began my faith journey and discovered my identity in God, it wasn't without difficulty or challenges. I would constantly hear whispers of lies that threatened to pull me back into old patterns of doubt and insecurity. I still struggle with this to this day, and I fear that it may be a never-ending battle, at least until it is my time to return to God. Those whispers sounded familiar; you're not good enough, you'll never be loved, you didn't do it right, and you failed again... Thankfully, faith gave me the weapons I needed to combat these lies. Prayer, scripture, and community are all tools I learned to wield against the enemy. These tools are what I used to replace falsehoods with God's truth; "I praise you, for I am wondrously made." (Psalm 139:14) "The Lord appeared to him from afar. I have loved you with an everlasting love; therefore I have continued my faithfulness in you." (Jeremiah 31:3) "even as he chose us in him before the foundation of the world, that we should be holy and blameless before him" (Ephesians 1:4) Might I recommend that when you are feeling down, close your eyes and recite these passages of scripture quietly, because each time I declared these truths over my life, these lies lost a little more power.

Now, I know you're sitting there asking me: "Brenton, how do I do this?" Well, it takes time, patience, and a willingness to meet God in the middle. I'm happy to give you some points to think about, which I will shortly, but you need to be willing to put in the work too. God, like any good father, has things that He wants to teach you. Education takes time and effort, and if you're not willing to take that step of faith and say yes to God by taking time out of your day to meet with Him, then you won't get much out of the advice I have for you.

Discovering what I have means developing a relationship with the One who created you. I invite you now, if you have not already done so, to pray the following prayer asking Jesus into your heart:

> *"Dear Jesus, thank you for everything you've done for me. I come before you now, humbly asking that you come into my life. I recognize that I need you in my life to guide me, to love me, to heal me. I confess my sins to you, and I ask for your forgiveness. I confess that you are Lord, that you died on the cross for my sins so that one day I can reunite with you and our Father in Heaven. Holy Spirit, I ask that you enter my life as well. Guide my heart in all the right ways, and keep me away from the bad influences of this world. Father God, please send me blessings that I might know you better each morning. In Your Holy Name I pray, Amen."*

Congratulations! I'm so happy for you! Now that you've accepted Jesus into your life, the real work begins. He is about to change your life for the better, but that also means that there will be some difficulty along the way. While you are learning and experiencing His love for the first time, you need help. Here are the five ways I've learned to fully lean into the faith to get as much out of it as I can.

1. Spend Time in Scripture

The Bible is filled with verses that speak to who we are in Christ. You must take the time to open the Bible, read it, and meditate on the truth that you are reading so that it can reshape how you see yourself.

2. Surround Yourself with Godly Community

This is an important one. One of the biggest reasons I've heard about people leaving the Church or not wanting to join is stereotypical, hypocritical, cliquey, and unwelcoming Christians. Truth holds power, and if you share your story and feel unwelcome, ignore it or find someplace else. Pray about it. God will lead you where you need to be. At the end of the day, you're there to find community, and if they're not supportive, then move on. However, it is vitally important that you do find community somewhere. Being on this journey alone is a very difficult uphill battle. Trust me, I know from experience. You need friends by your side, so make sure you go to Church weekly.

3. Engage in Prayer

I just said it in the last paragraph, but to maintain any good relationship, you need communication. So, TALK TO GOD! Speak to Him about your daily struggles, your issues with identity, or whatever else is on your mind. If you've had a great day with no complaints, check in with Him and say so. He wants to hear from you no matter what the situation. In good or in bad, you must speak with Him regularly. If it was a great day, thank Him. If it was a really bad day, ask Him to help you cope with it.

4. Practice Gratitude

As you make your initial push into this new journey, take a minute to think about the past and make some mental notes of times when you feel that God was there all along. Here comes a mind-twisting thought: God is not subject to time. He still sees you in your mother's womb right this very second, just as He is able to see you reading this book now. He knows who His children are. So there will be times when He already showed His love and care for you and for everything in your life. You've just got to think about it and be grateful. Gratitude shifts your focus from what you don't have to what you do have, and it can mean all the difference.

5. Journal Your Journey

Writing down your thoughts and prayers can help you process your feelings and track growth over time. This could mean a simple lined journal with no frills that you use or a daily devotional book. Either way, put pen to paper. It is very soothing to get it out of your mind and heart. Go to your local supermarket to the arts and crafts area. There, you will usually find an aisle with tons of writing journals; some are Christian-themed, and others have writing prompts in case you get stuck. Otherwise, bookstores like Barnes and Noble have great Faith and Inspiration sections where you can find these journals. And while you're there, make sure you pick up a fresh copy of the Holy Bible for the new journey.

The search for identity is a journey we all take. For some, it is easy, but for many, it's not. It also doesn't have to end with confusion or depression. Through faith, we discover a truth that doesn't waver: we are loved, valued, and chosen by God Himself. This identity isn't something we earn or achieve; it is a gift that we are free to take. As you continue on your own journey, I encourage you to lean far into God's love for you and let it redefine how you see yourself. You are His, and that is enough because, after all, the price He paid was with His blood.

Reflection Questions

1. What lies about your identity have you believed in the past?

2. How does knowing you are a child of God change the way you see yourself?

3. What steps can you take to root your identity more firmly in God's truth?

Devotional Thought

"But you are a chosen race, a royal priesthood, a holy nation, God's own people, that you may declare the wonderful deeds of him who called you out of darkness into his marvelous light." — 1 Peter 2:9

Reflect on what it means to be chosen and cherished by God. How can this truth shape the way you live?

Recommended Reading

- *"You Are Free: Be Who You Already Are"* by Rebekah Lyons

- *"Who Do You Think You Are?"* by Mark Driscoll

- *"Identity in Christ"* by Neil T. Anderson

Recommended Songs

- *"Made For More (Live)"* by Josh Baldwin feat. Jenn Johnson

- *"Who You Say I Am"* by Hillsong Worship

- *"No Longer Slaves"* by Bethel Music

Chapter 3

THE IMPACT OF A SINGLE-PARENT HOUSEHOLD

DEAR **Younger Me,**

There's so much I wish I could say to you right now—so many truths I wish I could gently place within your heart to guide you through the complexities of the life you're living. I understand that being the youngest child in a single-parent home has come with its own unique challenges, questions, and emotions. The quiet absence you feel each day has shaped the person you're becoming in ways you may not yet fully comprehend.

I remember clearly those moments when you stood in classrooms, looking around during Father's Day activities or family-themed events, realizing once again that your family looked different from most others. Those experiences often left you feeling exposed, uncertain, and deeply aware of what—or rather, who—was missing. Even your older siblings, who stepped up to help ease the burden on Mom and protected you fiercely, couldn't completely fill that void. Their strength, comfort, and reassurance helped tremendously, but deep down, you still wondered why your father chose absence over presence.

You've had questions in your heart that no child should have to carry: Why did he leave? Was it something about you? Could you have done anything differently to keep him in your life? Those unspoken questions have lingered quietly in your mind, affecting how you see yourself and how you relate to the people around you. They're heavy burdens for a young heart to bear, but I need you to understand this now: you did not cause his absence, and it does not reflect your worth. His choices were never yours to control.

Your mother, though carrying a weight that sometimes felt impossible, did everything within her power to create a home filled with love, safety, and stability. You've watched her closely, noticing the tiredness in her eyes and sensing the quiet struggles beneath her strong exterior. Her tireless commitment to your family meant working long hours, juggling multiple jobs, and making daily sacrifices. As the youngest child, you often felt helpless, wishing you could ease her burdens. You learned to remain quiet about your own needs, not wanting to add to her worries or responsibilities.

In many ways, your childhood has been marked by an unusual maturity and independence. You've learned earlier than most children how to take care of yourself, how to help around the house, and how to recognize the emotional needs of others—especially your mother. Yet this independence, valuable as it may be, also left you feeling isolated, often hesitant to reach out or rely on others. You developed an early belief that asking for help was a sign of weakness or inconvenience.

I want you to know now, from the perspective of someone who has walked many more years in your shoes, that your independence was both a gift and a survival mechanism. It taught you strength, responsibility, and perseverance, all of which are beautiful qualities. Yet, in your adulthood, you'll need to learn something just as important—how to trust others, how to be vulnerable, and how to accept support when it's offered. One day, you'll realize that leaning on others doesn't reflect weakness; rather, it reveals strength, wisdom, and humility.

I also know that, at times, you've struggled deeply with emotions toward your father, emotions that range from longing and sadness to anger and resentment. Those feelings are completely valid. Allow yourself permission to acknowledge them without guilt or shame. Eventually, you'll discover the power of forgiveness—not necessarily for his sake, but for your own healing and peace. Forgiveness doesn't erase the past, but it does free you from the heavy burden of bitterness.

While you navigate these complexities, remember that you have never been truly alone. Even in moments when loneliness felt overwhelming, God's presence surrounded you. Scripture reminds us clearly in *Psalm 68:5*:

"Father of the fatherless and protector of widows is God in his holy habitation."

This promise has always been yours. Even when the world seemed chaotic, uncertain, or unfair, He was quietly shaping your story, placing people in your life to show you love and care, and guiding you in subtle yet powerful ways.

Younger me, your experiences in a single-parent home have not been easy, but they've also equipped you in ways you might not yet realize. They've taught you empathy—giving you eyes to recognize pain in others and a heart that responds with compassion. They've cultivated resilience —enabling you to face challenges with determination and hope. And most importantly, they've drawn you closer to God, allowing you to discover firsthand the depth of His fatherly care.

You've also been blessed with older siblings who have stood by your side, offering strength, laughter, protection, and friendship. Though you're the youngest, your voice, your feelings, and your perspectives have always mattered deeply. You might sometimes have felt overlooked, yet your experiences and insights will one day powerfully impact those around you, helping others find strength, encouragement, and comfort in their own journeys.

As you continue to grow, please hold onto this truth tightly: your family, though different from others, was exactly the place you were meant to grow. Within this unique context, God planted seeds of strength, resilience, faith, and compassion that will bloom in incredible ways as you move forward.

You are more than the sum of your experiences. Your value is not diminished by your father's absence or defined by your family structure. Rather, your worth is securely anchored in God's perfect love. Your Heavenly Father sees you fully, loves you unconditionally, and has beautiful purposes planned specifically for your life. Embrace these truths deeply. Allow them to guide your steps, shape your identity, and inspire hope.

One day, you'll look back clearly, seeing the intricate ways God transformed the challenges of your childhood into sources of strength and inspiration. You'll see how He redeemed your pain, restored your heart, and gave purpose to every difficult moment. Until that day comes, hold tight to His promise that He is always with you, that He loves you immensely, and that your life and story have an incredible purpose.

With profound compassion, deep respect, and heartfelt encouragement,
Your Older Self

When I try to think back on my childhood, I find it hard to remember specific events or the details about them. I can clearly recall the unique realities that accompanied growing up in a single-parent household. After my father left, my mom eventually married my step-father, Bill. Their marriage lasted about 9 years until the situation required separation, at which point, my mom, Joshua, and I moved and became the single-parent household I describe. My sister Tiffany was married at this point and was out of the house. When we got settled, it became clear that Mom assumed dual roles—provider and caregiver, disciplinarian and comforter. A single parent is not intended to fill dual roles.

God's design for proper marriage takes into account the roles He has destined for parents. Fathers are expected to be the main providers and protectors, whereas mothers are expected to be the caregivers and comforters. This does not mean that these roles are for those parents only or that they can't overlap at all; it just means that there is a primary and secondary parent responsible for each role. The roles are symbiotic in nature. They complement each other. Each parent has an important role to play, and neither one is more important than the other because if either one breaks down, both become less effective. And our family dynamic was undeniably shaped by these circumstances.

Growing up with only my mother present gave me emotions and responsibilities beyond my years. Feelings of abandonment from my father were quietly simmering beneath the surface, not only for me, but also for Mom. He failed to fulfill his God-given responsibility, forcing Mom into a role she was never meant to fill. This cost her dearly, as she was unable to find respite from parenthood, hobbies to keep her entertained, or socialization to maintain her friendships. She was expected to be a mother at all times, and I remember seeing the exhaustion on her face when she got home from work every day.

I often felt different from my friends, who enjoyed activities and holidays with both parents present. Moments that were staples in my youth, such as father-child events, magnified my sense of difference. It made me feel exposed and vulnerable unnecessarily. But alongside those challenges came closeness. My brother and I bonded deeply, and I depended on him emotionally in ways that were perhaps uncommon for a child, namely one in my situation. Our home was marked by a special resilience—a quiet strength born from necessity.

There were also practical challenges. Mom worked extremely hard, at times juggling three jobs to support us. Work and responsibility were a never-ending reality for her, and she was rarely able to take a breath and enjoy herself. We never went on vacation because we couldn't afford it financially. Mom always found a way, though, so she liked to take random car trips all over the state. It may not have been Disney, but it was a momentary respite from our unique sense of "normal." It rested her and gave her the energy she needed to move forward, and that was all I cared about. I enjoyed taking these trips with her, of course. I think my favorite memory with my mom was when we attended a couple of free concerts at what is now known as the Maranatha Bible & Missionary Conference in Norton Shores, Michigan. We were able to enjoy hearing Selah and Charles Billingsley there, and it's a memory I'll never forget.

Sacrifices were commonplace in our house—mostly from her, but from us kids as well—yet she rarely voiced a complaint. I learned not to ask for a lot because we simply could not afford it with our limited resources. Yet, our home was overflowing with immense love and persistent hope. One thing she always made a priority when I was younger was youth group. Mom made sure that she had enough gas in the car to make it to Rockford so that I could attend youth group. Thanks to her, my relationship with the Lord grew deeper, and my faith grew stronger.

My relationship with my mom was all I had, so it was a positive one—however, it was complex. She provided unconditional love, yet at times, I could feel the tension of her exhaustion in the air, which inadvertently made me feel guilty about our situation. As I grew older, I experienced complicated emotions regarding my absent father. These times were frequent, but I usually kept them to myself. I didn't want attention, I didn't want sympathy, I just wanted answers. Anger and sadness intermingled, leaving me conflicted and uncertain about how to process my feelings. I sometimes assumed roles that were not expected of me, such as feeling responsible for issues beyond my control. Understanding these complexities was vital to finding healing later in life.

I experienced a heightened independence from a young age. I learned to care for myself, despite what my messy bedroom would have told you. The basics of waking up and getting off to school were my own responsibility, as mom was often gone by then. I usually walked to school since it was close by, mainly out of avoidance of the bus since I had issues with bullying and lack of ability to connect with people. My brother often came to sit with me while the bus driver came to make sure I didn't have any issues.

A less positive impact was evident in my struggle to trust others. My father's absence left me wary of depending too much on others. I was convinced that I would be let down. Friendships and relationships often felt unsafe. I kept emotional walls firmly in place, a fear response brought about by feelings that if I was vulnerable with another person, my trust would be broken, leaving me further abandoned. I remember having a crush on one of the girls in my history class. My history class was above the library, and windows were looking down into the computer lab underneath. I was going downstairs to the library to do some research for a class project, and a letter that she supposedly wrote was handed to me as I left the room.

I took a seat at a computer and read the letter. It spoke about how she felt the same way that I felt about her, and she asked if I was interested in a relationship. As I read the letter, I smiled to myself. But at that moment, I remember hearing laughing coming from the windows. I looked up to see the friend group she hung out with, laughing at me. I was embarrassed that I had been duped into believing something that I wanted to happen for once. I checked "yes" on the note, finished my research, and went back to class. I handed the note back to her, and to the group, I said something to the effect of: "I'm not stupid, and I knew this was fake." I attempted to play it off, giving a show of strength despite being heartbroken and ridiculed. It left me with yet another example of how I couldn't possibly trust anyone else with my heart. And that would stay with me into my late 20s and early 30s.

Questions of worth plagued me deeply. My childhood and adolescence were filled with these questions. Always being asked and never were they answered. I wondered if something about me had driven my dad away, and it created deep insecurities within me that lingered into adulthood. My perception was often distorted by these thoughts, and it made it difficult to accept acceptance or genuine love or trust, even when it was freely offered.

As I got older, I slowly came around to a point of realization. It wasn't until adulthood that I understood how deeply my father's absence affected me. At first, it was the small things—certain songs, movies, or witnessing another person's father-child interactions—each with the power to reopen wounds I'd assumed and hoped had healed. Understanding that these were triggers to my problems became the solution because healing begins with recognition. Instead of avoiding them or suppressing them like I did for so many years, I learned and began to acknowledge them. I named each of them out loud and allowed my mind to wander, prompting reflection and growth.

When I realized that I often avoided and suppressed these feelings, I recognized the time bomb that I was building within myself. This realization was only due to the reflection that I allowed myself to experience. I had hidden rage and anger built inside me, just waiting for an excuse to come out, and it honestly scared me. I still experience this on occasion, but it is only when I am honest with myself and the important people around me that the feeling subsides. Healing requires honesty, first with yourself and then with others. I masked the pain with a false outward confidence, and in doing so, I refused to openly acknowledge the lingering effects of my youth.

True progress began in my life when I openly grieved the loss of the traditional family experience, which was something I deeply desired to have. In my mind, this meant having the opportunity to express anger, sadness, and confusion without guilt or fear. Professional counseling in adulthood provided some essential guidance. Participating in therapy allowed me to unravel complex emotions, identify harmful patterns, and begin rewriting my narrative with intention and hope. Finding compassionate professionals who understood the unique struggle I was experiencing was critical to my emotional growth and healing.

As I started to heal, I slowly began to feel gratitude. I felt weird about it for a while, being that I learned these lessons during the hardest times of my life. How can I feel gratitude about something that took a lot of hurt to learn? Nonetheless, I came to deeply appreciate the qualities I learned in the crucible of my childhood—resilience, resourcefulness, independence, and, above all, compassion. These strengths are what now positively shape my adult life, relationships, and even how I parent my own kids.

When these qualities took a stronghold in my life, it was then that my admiration and appreciation for my mother deepened profoundly as I matured. Her determination and sacrifices, which once went unnoticed, became visible and meaningful. Her steadfastness taught me about unconditional love, quiet strength, and unwavering commitment. My appreciation for her and for who she was to me has only intensified since her passing. She wasn't just mom; she was my superhero. A protector during the hard times, and that dependable gentle hug when I needed it the most.

Losing her brought a deeper clarity to the life she provided my siblings and me through the immense sacrifices she made and the strength she constantly displayed. Her lasting legacy is her children, and I'm so proud of the three of us and who we've become. Not one of us is perfect, and each has their own quirks. We, without a doubt, positively impact all those around us. I know that is what she is most proud of. When she had to stand before God and give an account of her life, I know that she thanked Him for giving us to her, and then she immediately bragged about how proud she was of us, never once taking credit for herself. That's the kind of person she was, and I pray to the Lord that He reward her efforts. When my time comes, I cannot wait to see the rewards she achieved, despite knowing that she cast those rewards at His feet in worship. My mom loved Jesus, and thanks to her, so do I.

It was through these challenges, which I once only perceived as hardship, that I now recognize them for what they are: invaluable lessons that were essential in the formation of my character and resilience. They are what shaped me into the man that I am today. Importantly, my experiences motivated me to intentionally break negative family patterns. My childhood became purposeful, which is something I never would have imagined. It inspired deliberate decisions about my relationships, the parenting I provide to my kids, and especially my emotional health. After my mom's passing, I became even more determined to ensure her sacrifices would bear lasting fruit. My children's experiences, I vowed, would differ significantly from mine—not only to honor her legacy but to ensure that her love, strength, and commitment lived on. I made it my mission as a father to break generational cycles and create a healthier family legacy. A legacy that would make my mother deeply proud.

The single-parent home that I found myself in positioned me to embrace God as my father. Psalm 68:5 says: *"Father of the fatherless and protector of widows is God in his holy habitation."* This truth was something that surprised me when I read it for the first time. It was like God spoke to me directly through His word, and that is because He does. He wants us to read His word so that He can impart messages to us, so never neglect reading the Bible. When God filled those emotional gaps, He provided comfort, stability, identity, and unconditional acceptance. My reliance upon His faithfulness has anchored my identity and healed the deep wounds of fatherlessness.

My personal experiences have highlighted God's fatherly care in my life. At one point, what seemed clouded and obscured is now shining bright, and I'm amazed at how I missed it. In practical and emotional ways, there were provisions that defied all logic. There was comfort in moments of deep loneliness, and as I grew older, there was guidance in relational healing. My faith journey reinforced the reality that God is Our Father, all of us, you and me. His intimate care became central to my emotional healing and maturity.

As you continue down this road to healing within your story, you absolutely must surround yourself with healthy individuals. The time is over that you can be flippant with who you surround yourself with. To be successful, you have to set yourself apart and surround yourself with who you want to be and not who you were. Let me make this clear: these individuals who represent who you want to be are not perfect, so do not expect perfection. Rather, emulate them for the person they represent: God. Find other Christians to hang out with and find a church to attend because community and spiritual direction from a pastor is essential to your spiritual growth.

It was only when I surrounded myself with people who modeled commitment, healthy boundaries, and genuine care that I began to gain momentum. These relationships became trustworthy friends, and they offered safe spaces to practice vulnerability, which is a trust-building exercise. I learned to release those perfectionist expectations of others that were shaped by my experiences. I allowed grace and compassion to take over, which in turn reduced my anxiety, shame, and fear. It invited deeper emotional health and authentic connections into my life. Actively choosing new, healthy family patterns became empowering. Creating traditions, openly expressing love, and setting intentional relationship goals formed a new narrative that became a beautiful antidote to my childhood experiences.

Your family structure, though impactful, does not limit your potential. Embrace honesty. Pursue intentional healing. Allow faith to anchor your heart and not the pain. Above all, know that God is your father. He is Our Father, and He deeply loves you. He made you to be uniquely capable and powerfully equipped to create new, healthy family legacies. Your journey matters, and your future is filled with hopeful promise of a better tomorrow. Each sunrise is a new day. Seize it. Carpe Diem.

Reflection Questions

1. How has growing up in a single-parent household shaped your identity and relationships?

2. What positive strengths emerged from your family experience?

3. What steps could you take toward emotional healing that you can intentionally pursue today?

Devotional Thought

"Father to the fatherless and protector of widows is God in his holy habitation." Psalm 68:5

Recommended Reading

- *Fathered by God* by John Eldridge

- *The Father Heart of God* by Floyd McClung

Recommended Songs

- *"Good Good Father"* by Chris Tomlin

- *"Lean on Me"* by Kirk Franklin

Chapter 4

BUILDING A STRONG RELATIONSHIP WITH GOD

D^{EAR} Me,
　I know how hard it feels right now, carrying so much and not knowing where to lay it down. You've been searching for something solid, something you can trust, because everything around you feels fragile. Relationships break, plans fail, and sometimes, you question your self-worth. You've been longing for something more, something unshakable. What you're looking for, though you may not realize it yet, is a relationship with God.

I understand your hesitation. God feels distant, doesn't He? You wonder how someone so powerful and holy could care about someone like you. You've prayed, especially in times of desperation, but it feels like you were talking into the void. You've heard about God's love, but you don't know what it looks like or how it could possibly fill the emptiness you feel. These doubts and hesitations are normal, and I want you to know that building a relationship with God isn't an instant transformation; it's a journey that is taken one step at a time.

The first thing that I want you to know is that God is already pursuing you. Long before you ever thought about Him, He thought about you. He has seen your struggles, your pain, your sin, and your questions, and He is waiting, Not with judgment, but with open arms. This relationship isn't something you have to earn. It is a gift that He is offering freely. All He asks in return is that you freely choose to take a step toward Him.

It begins with trust, and I know trust hasn't come easily to you. How can it, when the man who was supposed to protect and guide you wasn't there when you needed him the most? God is not like anyone else you've known. He doesn't break promises, and He doesn't walk away. He's the kind of Father who stays through every storm, who carries you when you're too tired to keep going.

The beauty of this relationship is that it doesn't depend on you being perfect or having it all together. God isn't waiting for you to clean yourself up before you come to Him. He wants you as you are: messy, broken, and full of questions. He's not afraid of your doubts or your fears. He doesn't demand blind faith from you. He is happy to help you find the answers to those questions that you have. In fact, He welcomes them because He knows they're part of the process of building trust.

I wish I could show you the moments ahead, the moments where you'll feel His presence so clearly that it will bring tears to your eyes. I wish I could tell you how His life will begin to heal the deepest wounds in your heart, the ones you've tried so hard to ignore and mend on your own. But these moments will come in time, and they'll be even more meaningful because of the journey it takes to get there.

You will learn to talk to Him, not in polished prayers, but in honest ones… "God, I'm hurting," or "God, I'm lost, and I don't know what to do. Please help me." You'll learn to listen for His responses, the ones that come not from a booming voice from the sky but from a whisper in your heart. Responses that bring peace and clarity, not more confusion. Over time, these conversations will become the foundation of your relationship with Him.

There will be times when this relationship feels one-sided when you wonder if God is still watching over you. In those moments, I want you to remember that relationships grow through perseverance. Even when you can't feel Him, He's still working. Even when you doubt Him, He's still holding you.

This isn't about religion or rules. It's about connection. It's about finding the One who knows you completely and loves you fully. It's about discovering that the void you've been trying to fill on your own can only be filled by Him. The religion and rules part comes later when you find a church to call your community. Take the first step. Open your heart, even just a little, and let Him in. Trust that He is for you, not against you. Trust that He wants to build something within you that will stand firm in the test of time, no matter what life throws your way.

One day, you'll look back and see how every small prayer, every moment of faith, was building something beautiful: a relationship with God that will sustain you in ways you never thought possible. And you'll realize that what started as a hesitant step forward became the greatest relationship of your life.

With Love and Hope,
Your Older Self

In a previous chapter, I led you through the prayer to invite Jesus into your life. If that was the first time you've ever said that prayer and invited Him in, I just want to share again how happy I am for you. The journey you've just begun will be filled with twists and turns, and there will be difficulty, but it will all be worth it. I promise. Building a relationship with God is unlike any other relationship you'll ever have. It's not about proximity, shared interests, your favorite color, or even what you can offer; It's about connection, trust, and intimacy with the One who created you.

For those of us who have wrestled with fatherlessness, this relationship can feel foreign at first. How do you build trust with someone you can't see, hear, or feel the way you could a person? How can you relate to God as a Father when your earthly father left such a void? These definitely are questions that I wrestled with, and I'm sure you are too. As we spend time together in this chapter, we will explore how to cultivate that connection and how to experience the transformative love of God in a way that fills the void no human ever could.

God is One Being, but He chooses to manifest Himself into three persons: The Father, The Son, and The Holy Spirit. Each is distinct from each other but equal in divinity. This is what many Christians will call the Mystery of the Trinity. Do not worry; I'm no theologian, so I won't dive deep into these questions, and there won't be quizzes. I will leave that to those significantly more learned than I am, but it is important to know because I want to point out the relationship of Father and Son. In the Book of Genesis, God says that He made us in His Image. Fatherhood, as we deeply desire to experience it, is modeled after Him! So, to answer the questions I asked a paragraph ago: We can both build trust and relate to God as a Father because He is the source and creator of Fatherhood itself.

Growing up without a father, the concept of God as a "Heavenly Father" felt both comforting and confusing. On one hand, it was reassuring to think of a God who cared for me in ways my earthly father couldn't. On the other hand, it was hard to trust the idea of a father when my only reference point had been absent, leaving me disappointed.

The turning point came when I realized that God isn't just a better version of an earthly father. He is so much more! He is the perfect Father, one who loves unconditionally, provides endlessly and never abandons. This realization didn't come all at once, of course. It was a gradual process of unlearning the fears and insecurities I had associated with the word "father" and replacing them with the truth of who God is.

As with any relationship, trust is the cornerstone and foundation, but it is of special importance in our relationships with God. Yet, trust doesn't come easily when you've been let down before. For a long time, I held back from fully trusting God, and I still do. Friends, I'm not perfect. I held back because I was afraid He would disappoint me the way others already had done. I prayed, but I didn't fully open my heart. I believed in Him, but only with caution.

Allow me to quickly address something here for just a moment. Beginning a new relationship with God does not mean that you have a magical answer to everything you could possibly want. God will not give you something that you do not need. How many times have we all prayed that we would win the lottery? I know I have. Imagine that life-changing moment from His perspective. He just granted your prayer, and you're delivered a wheelbarrow full of cash. What is the first thing you're going to do with it? If your answer was anything other than giving every penny away, not keeping a single cent for yourself, then you're not trusting that God can provide for you.

The point that I'm trying to make here is that between trusting in Him and leading a fruitful life, you will need to be disciplined, focused, frugal, and resourceful. You can't just live an undisciplined life, squandering away your blessings and expecting that God is going to come in at the last moment to save you like something out of Hollywood. God is a good Father, and with that comes teaching moments. He will gladly allow you to fall on your face if the situation you're in was entirely of your own doing. He will use it to teach you and mold you into a responsible lifestyle. I know that sounded rough, but that was the point.

When I realized this, after my moments of foolishness, I prayed a simple prayer. "God, help me trust You." It's not full of theological thought, but it was honest. God doesn't need you to recite some fancy prayer. He just needs you to be willing to learn from Him. When I said this prayer, I noticed that my thoughts changed. I no longer went out of my way to grab a "lottery ticket." Over time, God answered that prayer by showing me His faithfulness in small, meaningful ways. A verse that spoke to my heart, or a prayer that was answered unexpectedly. The sense of peace came from simply sitting in His presence and not being antsy to check the box off my list. Trust doesn't happen all at once, but step-by-step, God showed me that He was worthy of my trust.

Prayer is the lifeline of a relationship with God. It's how we talk to Him, share our hearts, and listen for His guidance. For many of us, however, prayer can feel intimidating or awkward at first. What do you say to the Creator of the universe? How do you know He's listening? I've had this doubt in my mind often. My advice is to ask Him to send confirmation. By confirmation, I do not mean that the heavenly realms open, and a dove flies down to land on your shoulder. What I mean is a humble and simple request that you're on the right track with your prayer. If He approves of the confirmation, you will know it when you see it. You will feel it in your heart and just know.

For quite a while, I felt that prayer had to be formal and perfect, much like a well-rehearsed speech. I've learned, however, that God much prefers a simple conversation. It's raw, honest, and real. Sometimes, it's full of words because there is a lot to say, while other times, you sit in silence waiting to hear God speak to you. Regardless, the most important thing to do is simply to show up, even if you don't know what to say. God can see what is in your heart before you even think of talking to Him about it. Just go to Him, and everything will be fine.

One of the questions I hear often is how to know if God is speaking to you. First things first, when God speaks to you, more often than not, it will be a quiet whisper. He prefers not to use His "dad voice," at least if you're listening and being obedient. If not, your chest might rattle a little bit, like mine has on occasion. I know you're thinking I'm crazy, but I'm being serious. This is a real experience that I've felt. I digress, but you're more likely to experience His voice in the form of a nudge in your spirit, a verse that resonates deeply with you for some reason, or a sense of peace about a decision. The process for me to learn to recognize His voice meant I had to tune in and pay attention. You will quickly learn what silence is and what it feels like when something is different.

I won't forget the first morning I started by spending time in His Word, specifically the Book of Proverbs. It was a quiet morning. I had just woken up and felt the stillness of the day as the early morning light was shining through my window. As I walked to the kitchen to start a pot of coffee, I felt a strong push in my heart to read Proverbs. I pulled a U-turn, grabbed my Bible out of my bedroom, and went back to making coffee as I read. I ended up reading the entire Book of Proverbs in a couple of hours. If you're not familiar, the Book of Proverbs is a book of wisdom. Full of wise sayings, it offers guidance on how to live a good life. The main idea being that being obedient to God's Will is the main path to wisdom and righteousness. I highly recommend that you participate in a reading plan that takes you through the Holy Bible in a year. You will uncover so much general knowledge and understanding that you'll be surprised how much your eyes open to His Word.

His voice is most clearly revealed in His Word. The Holy Bible is more than just a book. It is a conversation. I also learned to listen in prayer, to quiet my thoughts, and to let Him speak. Over time, I realized that God's voice often comes through the people, circumstances, and stillness around me. A word of caution, though. If you've asked Jesus into your heart, you're now a child of God. This is a beautiful thing, but in doing so, you've made an enemy. Satan prowls the earth, seeking the ruin of souls. The entire purpose of Satan is to separate us from God, and he will do everything within his power to cause us to trip and stumble in our walk with the Lord.

Satan is the exact opposite of God; he is filled with pure greed, anger, and complete hatred of humans because we were made in God's image, whereas the angels were not, Satan included. That is why Satan rebelled against God. So, when you're praying, here is some advice. If you think you're hearing the voice of God, compare what is said to you with the scripture. If what was said is consistent with the Word, it is God. Still use caution though, because Satan knows the scripture too. He tempted Jesus by misquoting scripture. If you have even the slightest doubt, consult a brother or sister in Christ or your Pastor for help. This is where being connected to the community, as I mentioned earlier, is so important. It provides a resource for you should you find yourself needing help.

Outside of Satan, there is also the chance that you're hearing your own conscience. Therefore, pray to the Lord and the Holy Spirit that you be granted the gift of discernment to see through the lies of the enemy or confusion.

Obedience. That is where we will all stumble. I know I have plenty of time, and I will continue to do so. That being said, "By this, everyone will know that you are my disciples if you love one another." It is not only by our belief and faith in the Lord but also by our lives and how we live them. Jesus routinely used the metaphor that we are the fruit, and He is the vine. To bear good fruit means to be obedient and remain in the faith. Obedience is an act of love and trust, a way of saying, "God, I believe Your way is better than mine." Obedience is difficult, especially when it calls us to step outside our comfort zones. I've learned that obedience often starts with small steps. Saying yes to God in the little things prepares us to say yes to the big things. Each act of obedience deepens our relationship with Him and strengthens our faith.

I don't want you to feel powerless in your fight against sin. It is a constant war, and you will lose some battles. It is in those moments that God wants you the most. He wants you to bring yourself to Him so that He can stand you up, dust you off, humbly confess and ask Him for forgiveness, and move on. He does not want you to wallow in self-pity because you've failed Him, because you haven't. To fail God is to give up and say: "Well, I've sinned, and now I'm doomed to Hell. I guess I give up." Friends, when we make mistakes, it is difficult to confess those, apologize, and ask forgiveness. I get it, trust me. It is vitally important to recognize that this is the precise moment that God is calling out the weaker parts of us to strengthen us. If we humbly ask for forgiveness, that is, actually be sorry for the sins we've committed, He will forgive us those sins, and He will cast the memory of those sins away "as far as the East is from the West, so far does he remove our transgressions from us." (Psalm 103:12)

A strong relationship with God requires a solid foundation. For most Christians, that is built upon three pillars: His Word, prayer, and community. These three elements become the anchors that keep us steady during the storms of life and keep us grounded in times of doubt. His Word is the Holy Bible, and it is the ultimate guide for understanding who God is and how He works in our lives. This does not mean that the Bible is your only source. Research whatever it is that you are interested in, review other translations, and look into what the Church fathers said about the topic.

How many times have you heard someone say: "I wish Heaven had a phone so I can talk to God…" Well, guess what? Prayer is the phone! It is that communication with God that keeps our relationship alive and growing. Surrounding yourself with other believers provides encouragement, accountability, and support. This is why community is essential.

As your relationship with God grows, you will begin to notice changes in life. There will be peace that replaces anxiety, joy that comes from knowing you are loved, and a sense of purpose that gives life direction. These changes don't happen overnight but are gradual fruits of walking closely with God. God's love transformed how I saw myself and others. It filled the void left by fatherlessness and gave me a sense of belonging that I had never known. Building my relationship with God didn't erase my struggles, but it gave me God's strength to face them with hope, and it made all the difference.

Building that relationship with Him is a journey, not a destination. It is about showing up, trusting Him, and letting Him lead you step by step. Wherever you are in your faith journey, know that God is ready to meet you where you are and draw you closer to His heart. He will leave the ninety-nine to find the one. It is the most profound love I've ever come to experience, and I'm so thankful for Him. I pray that you get to experience this as well. I don't know your personal story or the tragedies you've faced up until now, but I am confident that God will be able to heal your heart if you let Him. Start walking this path today, and see the blessings that it brings in your life.

Reflection Questions

1. What does building a strong relationship with God look like in your life right now?

2. Where do you struggle most—trust, prayer, obedience, or something else? Pray about them.

3. How can you take one step today to grow closer to Him?

4. What does the word "father" mean to you? How has your perception of earthly fathers influenced your view of God?

Devotional Thought

"Draw near to God, and He will draw near to you..." — James 4:8

Reflect on what it means to draw near to God and how He promises to respond.

Practical Step

Each day, spend increasing time in silent reflection, asking God to speak to your heart. Begin with 5 minutes, increasing each day by 5 minutes until you reach an hour. During this time, you may silently read His Word or just sit quietly in silent contemplative prayer. It is up to you. Keep a journal of what you sense Him saying to you, sharing it with a brother or sister in Christ or your Pastor.

Key Insight

In prayer, God doesn't require or even want perfect words. He wants your authentic heart, all baggage included. Show Him all of you by being vulnerable, being humble, asking for healing, and being ready to be amazed at what He does for you. He is merciful, more than we can possibly fathom.

Recommended Reading

- *"Crazy Love"* by Francis Chan

- *"The Pursuit of God"* by A.W. Tozer

- *"Prayer: Experiencing Awe and Intimacy with God"* by Timothy Keller

Recommended Songs

- *"Draw Me Close to You"* by Michael W. Smith

- *"Reckless Love"* by Cory Asbury

- *"Good Good Father"* by Chris Tomlin

Chapter 5

EXPERIENCING GOD'S LOVE

Hey Bubba,

I know you've heard these words before—*God loves you*. People say it in church, in passing, and even in songs you've listened to, but it feels empty and distant. Inside your heart, you struggle to believe it. It's like a blanket statement applying to everyone but you because somehow it skipped over you. You wonder how a God so vast, so powerful, could love *you*. Not just humanity as a whole, but *you*—with all your flaws, fears, sins, and the silent ache you carry inside, deep-seated in your chest. It makes everything feel so heavy. If God's love is real, why do you feel so distant from it? Why does it feel like something reserved for others but never fully reaching you? I know how hard it's been to believe in love, real love. A love that stays, the kind that doesn't leave when you fail or don't measure up.

I wish I could sit with you and tell you everything I've come to understand. And I guess, in a way, I am. But I wish I could look you in the eyes and say: "You are already fully loved." Not because of anything you have done or failed to do, not because you have to earn it, but because that's who God is. His love isn't something you strive for; it's something He freely gives. I know that hearing those words isn't enough. You need to *experience* that love, not just be told about it, and that's where your journey truly begins. This is where you will begin to trust in Him and trust in the love He provides. I know this isn't enough for you right now. Just hearing these words doesn't make them true. Even so, how can you believe in something you've never truly felt?

The purpose I have for you in reading this is because I want to tell you how I got to where I am now—how I moved from *knowing about* God's love to *experiencing* it. Because when I did, everything changed. The way I saw you in the mirror, the way I saw life, the way I handled pain, and the way we carried ourselves every day. It all shifted when I finally let God in, and I want that for you more than anything.

Before I truly experienced God's love, I spent years searching for something to fill that void inside my heart. You know the void well—the emptiness that lingers after another disappointment, another breakup, another letdown, another betrayal, and those days when you wonder why Dad isn't around to talk about this stuff. So, you did what many others did in the same situation; you tried to fill it yourself.

You tried to fill it with people, romantic and not, hoping that: "If I can just find someone to love me enough, maybe I'll be satisfied." You sought love from your girlfriends, and yes, that included promiscuity. You're not proud of it like many men are because, in your eyes, it's a stain on your reputation. It led to even more heartbreak, heartbreak that still lingers to this day in your current relationship. It's not hopeless romanticism or a desire to return to them. Rather, it's the desire to fix what you have broken. This sting is more the pain of knowing you were part of making another girl's life just as broken as yours. You know that hurt people, hurt people. And with the pain you've felt and the high standards you end up holding yourself to, you just can't forgive yourself for that.

You will spend many nights laying awake wondering: "When I find the girl God has planned for me, how could she even stand to look at such a broken human being and be happy?" "How can she know that my heart is in the right place despite it not being in the right place on so many occasions before?" "Who are you to think you can be trusted like this again?" "You're not worthy of the love of a Daughter of God. Don't kid yourself. Just give up."

This self-imposed torture seemed to be your penance. Just punishment for causing more pain in the lives of others. It lingers for a few years, becoming a major part of our mental health journey, but it slowly recedes as you learn more about who God is and what He is all about, and about who the enemy is and what his objective is for God's people. God is the provider of the purest form of love, of redemption, of forgiveness, and of reconciliation.

You also tried filling the void with general friendships, but you always found yourself to be socially awkward. You attempted to get to know other people, but the clash of your personality with others was always an obstacle. Trying to cultivate these friendships was like pouring water into a broken jar. It eventually all leaked out, leaving you just as empty as before, but each time, it slowly eroded your self-esteem and self-worth. So, you ended up a lone wanderer, doing whatever you wanted to do when you wanted to do it. It becomes a hard thing to change about yourself later when you start a family because when you go from one end of the spectrum to the other, it is quite the learning curve. It was exhausting to experience, but you are glad you did.

You need to learn to feel these emotions: the exhaustion of chasing love that always seemed out of reach, the frustration of never quite being enough, and the loneliness of feeling unseen. But here's what I've learned: the love you are searching for, the love you ache and desire for more than anything else—it was never meant to come from people alone. The love you need, the love you are searching for, and the love that *can* fill the void comes only from the One who made you. Brenton, just like every other human being on the face of this planet, you are fearfully and wonderfully made. God created you with a plan in mind, with a purpose, and with love so vast you cannot fully comprehend it in this plane of existence.

What about all the other stuff I mentioned? That was the work of the devil. A fallen angel who rejected the will of God and desires only one thing: to steal, kill, and destroy anything he possibly can. The eternal destination of the devil is Hell, an eternal separation from God, and he wants to take as many humans as he can with him. He knows he is defeated; he just wants to spread the pain and anguish. Keep your eyes fixed on God because if you do, the devil will not win the war, maybe a battle or two, but not the war.

I have already told you the story of when I accepted God into my heart. That was a single moment in time that I can point to, but other than that, I can't tell you the other moments when things changed. The small steps in the right direction. These were several moments in time—whispers of love so quiet that I almost missed them because I was too busy searching elsewhere, trying to figure it out on my own. Spoiler alert—when you walk with Jesus, you are never alone.

It was the moment I felt peace in the middle of heartbreak that I knew it had to come from something greater than myself. Because despite the heartbreak, I had an uncomfortable sense of comfort. It was like I wasn't supposed to feel the comfort, but with that feeling came reassurance. Romans 8:38-39: *"For I am sure that neither death, nor life, nor angels, nor principalities, nor things present, nor things to come, nor powers, nor height, nor depth, nor anything else in all creation, will be able to separate us from the love of God in Christ Jesus our Lord."* It was the moment that I read these words that I realized that nothing, not my mistakes, not my doubts, not my sins, not even the deepest wounds in my heart, have the power to separate me from God's love. Nothing. And it was at this moment that I cried out to God, releasing the painful frustration and anger, only to feel an overwhelming sense of His presence, a reminder that He was listening and that He wasn't leaving.

God's love is not something you achieve.
It's not something you chase as if you're in a marathon.
It's something you *receive*.

His love had been there all along, but I had been too afraid to receive it. I thought I had to make myself better first, as if I had to earn it somehow. But that was the biggest lie I had ever believed. Any guesses on where that whispered lie came from? Yes, the devil. When I realized that and eventually let go of my pride, fear, need to control everything, need to learn and understand everything, His love poured in like a flood, filling every broken part of me and overflowing my heart and mind.

The problem with love in this fallen world is that it is often conditional. You have seen that. People love you when you meet their expectations, say the right things, and fit into the image they have of you. The moment you expand outside of those conditions, the love fades away.

God's love? It's the complete opposite.
God doesn't love you because of what you do.
God doesn't love you only when you succeed.
God doesn't love you less when you sin or when you fail.

God's love is steady, unchanging, and unshakable. You could run as far as you wanted, and He would still be right there. You could make every mistake imaginable, and He would still call you His child. You can scream at Him, question Him, and doubt Him. I know I have. And you know what? He would still whisper *I love you. I am here, and I am not going anywhere.* I used to think that I had to clean myself up before coming to Him, like a child who spilled chocolate milk on their clothes and was afraid of being scolded. But God isn't like that. He isn't waiting for you to "fix" yourself, as if you even could. He wants you now, just as you are.

You don't have to take my word for it. You can experience His love for yourself. It begins with one simple step: *Let him in!*

Here are a few ideas for you:

1. **Be honest with Him**—You don't have to say the "right" words. Just talk to Him. Tell Him what you're feeling, what you're afraid of, what you need, and what you want. And guess what? If you don't know what to say, that's okay! Just sit with Him in silence. You'd be surprised by what promptings you get in your heart and mind.

2. **Ask Him to Show You His Love**—Pray this simple prayer with me: *God, I want to know Your love. I don't just want to hear about it anymore. I want to feel it and experience it for myself. Please show me Your love in a way I can understand. I love You, Father. Amen.*

3. **Look for His Love Every Day**—Sometimes, God's love surrounds us, and we don't even see it. It is revealed in the quiet moments. A sunrise or sunset. A song that seems to come on the radio at just the right time. A random scripture that came to mind that speaks directly to your heart. You've got to pay attention—He speaks more often than you realize. Here's a hint, though: He prefers *not* to use His "Dad" voice. He likes to whisper, so silence helps.

4. **Let Go of the Lies You've Believed**—If you have believed that you were unworthy of love, that you have to earn God's affection, or that He is distant from you, let those lies go. They are not from Him. They are from the devil. One thing you will need to learn is how to know who is speaking and discern if it is coming from Him. A great way is a simple prayer: "*Holy Spirit, breathe the truth into my mind. I'm confused. Please help me.*" Another great tool in discernment is His Word. Open the Holy Bible, read what it says, and if you're not sure, use the index to find passages of scripture that speak on the topic in your mind. If what is written in the scriptures doesn't seem to line up with what came to mind, you know it came from the devil because he likes to confuse and misquote scripture in order to deceive.

5. **Be Humble & Spend Time with Him**—Read His Word. Worship. Sit in silence and let Him speak to your heart. His love is everywhere —You just have to take the time to see it. Also, He *is* Truth. What you hear from Him may not sit well with you. Humility is required. We are His fallen creation and need to be in tune with *Him*, not the other way around.

I won't tell you that experiencing God's love means suddenly being perfect with sunshine and rainbows. It won't. There will be times when you still will struggle, there will still be pain along the way, there will still be moments of doubt, and there will be moments where you have to correct yourself. But I can promise you this: His love will be the one thing that never leaves you. The one thing in your life that never fades away.

It will heal you in ways you never thought possible. It will comfort you in the moments you feel most alone. It will remind you, again and again, that you belong to *Him*. His Son paid the ransom for your life *with His blood.* The blood Jesus Christ shed on the Cross has the power to forgive our sins and reconcile us with the Father if we accept it. It is a free gift with only one condition: We choose *Him*, and we forsake what the world offers us, accepting His love (and His corrections).

Brenton, stop running, stop striving, stop searching in places that will only leave you empty. Open your heart. Let Him in. Let yourself be loved by the One who *is* love and who has been loving you all along. Because once you do, you'll never be the same.

With all the love in *His* heart,
Your Older Self

For much of my life, I longed for love in its purest form, the kind that was unwavering, unconditional, and unshakable. But without a father present, love often felt like something I had to earn, something that could be withdrawn if I failed to measure up. I looked for it in people, in achievements, and in approval, but no matter how much I grasped for it, nothing ever seemed to fill the void.

It wasn't until I experienced the love of God that I truly understood what love was meant to be. His love wasn't transactional, wasn't dependent on my performance, and wasn't subject to change. It was steady, eternal, and unlike anything I had ever known. This chapter is about discovering and experiencing the love of God in a way that transforms your heart, brings healing, and fills the void left by fatherlessness. It's about learning that His love is not just something we hear about. It's something we can know personally and deeply.

There's a vast difference between knowing about God's love and actually experiencing it. I had heard for years that God loved me, but for much of my life, it felt like just a concept, a theological truth that I agreed with but didn't feel. The turning point came when I allowed myself to be vulnerable to God. When I stopped running, stopped striving, and simply received His love as it was, without trying to earn it, without questioning whether I deserved it.

What I realized was that God's love is not conditional. It doesn't fluctuate based on my actions. God's love is not distant. It is intimate and personal. And finally, God's love is not like human love. It doesn't fail, fade, or leave. Experiencing God's love isn't about doing more. It's about surrendering and letting Him love you as you are. Sometimes, the biggest obstacle to experiencing God's love is not God Himself. It's us. Our wounds, our past experiences, and our misconceptions about love can all create barriers that make it hard to truly receive what He freely gives. Some common barriers are feeling unworthy, having a deep-seated fear of rejection, and comparing God's love to human love.

If you've been abandoned, rejected, or made to feel like you're not enough, it's easy to assume that God's love works the same way. The truth is God's love is not based on worthiness; it's based on who He is. (Romans 5:8). The fear of rejection is a real anxiety these days because when people have walked away from us, we might assume that God will too. But in Deuteronomy 31:8 it states: "It is the Lord who goes before you; He will be with you, He will not fail you or forsake you; do not fear or be dismayed."

And finally, when we compare how we as humans love one another to how God loves us, we can be thrown off a bit. When our experience with love has been painful, insensitive, forced, or unfriendly, we may feel that God's love will be the same. Thankfully, that is not the truth of the matter. Whereas the love that humans feel is modeled after God's love, it's not perfect like God's love is. 1 Corinthians 13:4-7 says: "Love is patient and kind; love is not jealous or boastful; it is not arrogant or rude. Love does not insist on its own way; it is not irritable or resentful; it does not rejoice at wrong but rejoices in the right. Love bears all things, believes all things, hopes all things, endures all things." This is God's definition of love. Let it enter our hearts and shape how we interact with others. By breaking down these barriers, we allow God to heal the wounds that have distorted our view of Him.

You may have attended a philosophy class where the concept of love was broken down into Greek form. This is where they introduce the concept and definition of how the Greeks defined love based on which words they used. There is agape, eros, philia, storge, philautia, and xenia. Let's briefly explore how these break down in case you aren't familiar with them or need a refresher.

Agape love is that of unconditional love, that is, the love of God for person and of person for God. Eros is love of intimate nature, the love of spouses for one another. Philia is brotherly love or love for friends and community. Storge is rarely used but means specifically the love of family. It is used to describe love between parents and their children. Philautia is self-love. I feel that philautia is self-explanatory, but it also carries the idea that you also regard your own happiness or advantage.

The Greeks split this one into both positive and negative attributes depending on the context because whereas looking out for yourself is important and would be looked at positively, going down the road of egotism would use the same word but with a negative connotation. And finally, xenia is hospitality or guest-friendship. It describes things like generosity and hospitality for guests and foreigners.

As we can see, love can be defined by humans in numerous ways, but God is the original author. Experiencing God's love isn't just an emotional feeling. It's something we see in action. Throughout my journey, I began recognizing God's love through His provision, His grace, and His presence. Even when I felt alone, God always made a way for me, whether through unexpected opportunities, friendships, or moments of peace when I needed it the most. He provided for me when I couldn't. Trusting Him in these moments was difficult, but having faith that He would move when it was time was the tool I needed.

Through the years, and especially since I've left military service, I've struggled with mental health. Anxiety, depression, and symptoms of Post-Traumatic Stress Disorder (PTSD), coupled with a traumatic brain injury, caused issues with employment. Thankfully, the Veteran's Affairs helped me, and through lots of therapy, both physical and mental, I'm able to feel almost like me again. Nonetheless, those moments were the most desperate, and God was watching to catch me if I fell.

Also, in those moments of desperation was a version of me that was not pleasant. My faith and love for God was mostly internal, and I would lash out in anger at others. I would say or do things selfishly in desperate attempts to fix myself, hurting other people in the process. No matter how many mistakes I made, He was always there, and His love never wavered. He didn't love me any less on my worst days or more on my best days. He didn't care that at some times I was mad at Him for allowing me to experience this pain because He knew that the new version of me that He was building would be thankful for it.

In the moments of pain, confusion, and loneliness, He was always nearby. I spoke of this in the first chapter, when, in my room, in the dark of night, I would fall asleep and cry. As they say, hindsight is 20/20. I look back and can see it all in a positive light, despite the sadness and heartache that was present at the time. His presence made all the difference. I felt Him near in ways I cannot explain. God's love is not passive. It actively pursues us and restores us.

The Bible is filled with stories that highlight God's love, and one of the most powerful is the parable of the prodigal son. (Luke 15:11-32) If you aren't familiar, the parable tells the story of a wealthy man with two sons; the younger son asks his father for his share of the inheritance. In these days, this was not a good thing. Inheritance was given upon death, much like it's expected to today, but back then, doing this was basically telling his father that he was dead to him. His father divided the property as his son asked. He took what his father gave him and left. He squandered all he had in a short time, living in debauchery. Eventually, the money ran out, and he could no longer live as he was. He went and began working for another and soon realized that his life with his father was much better than what he thought and how he was living then. So, he decided to return home, tail between his legs, to beg his father to accept him back. He was going to offer his father his labor as if he were a servant. But, when he returned to his father's house, his father saw him coming and welcomed him back with open arms. His father quickly dressed him in fine clothing and jewelry. His son was lost, but now he is found.

This emulates exactly how God will love us: Unconditionally. Even in our mistakes, weaknesses, and confusion, He will love us unconditionally. He will restore us to our place and welcome us home. No matter how far we wander, how broken we feel, or how much we doubt we deserve it, God's love remains.

One of the hardest lessons I had to learn was that God's love is not something to be achieved. It's something to rest in. A deeper experience in God's love is what will make you feel more comfortable with this. By no means am I perfect in the strictest sense for these recommendations, as I struggle with the rest of the Christian population, but they are still great to focus on should you need help:

1. Spend Time in His Presence

Prayer isn't just about requests. It's about sitting with God, talking to Him honestly, and allowing Him to fill the empty spaces in your heart. It's also about giving Him praise where it is due. Other times, it is appropriate to just open prayer time with a simple statement like: "God, I just wish to sit with you in silence. Please speak to me if there is something I should know."

2. Meditate on Scripture About His Love

- Romans 8:38-39 – Nothing can separate us from God's love

- 1 John 4:9-10 – God showed His love by sending Jesus

- Zephaniah 3:17 – God delights in us and sings over us

3. Recognize His Love in Everyday Life

Sometimes, God's love shows in the simplest of ways: the sunrise, a kind word from a stranger, a random feeling of peace. It is important to think of the times when this happened and take note of it in a journal.

4. Let Go of Guilt and Shame

Extremely important is the fact that God's love is not limited by our past. He sees us fully and still calls us His own. God uses the least likely people to accomplish His plans. Paul the Apostle, formerly named Saul of Tarsus, authorized the execution of Christians until an encounter with Jesus Himself. While He felt guilt and shame for his actions, He took the assignment Jesus presented to him and converted to Christianity.

For such a long time, I searched for love in all the wrong places, believing that nothing could fill the space left by my father's absence. But I was wrong. God's love is the only love that never leaves, never fades, and never fails. It's a love that reaches into the deepest wounds and brings healing. If you've struggled to experience God's love, I want to encourage you: He is not far from you. He is closer than you think, waiting for you to simply receive what He has already given.

You are loved not because of what you do but because of who He is.

Reflection Questions

1. Have you ever struggled to believe in God's love for you? What made it difficult?

2. In what ways has God already shown His love in your life?

3. What is one step you can take to rest in His love more fully?

Devotional Thought

"See what love the Father has given us, that we should be called the children of God; and so we are. The reason why the world does not know us is that it did not know him." — 1 John 3:1

God's love is not rationed—it is *lavished* upon us. Let yourself receive it.

Recommended Reading

- *"The Ragamuffin Gospel"* by Brennan Manning

- *"The Furious Longing of God"* by Brennan Manning

- *"Abba's Child"* by Brennan Manning

Recommended Songs

- *"How He Loves"* by David Crowder Band

- *"Reckless Love"* by Cory Asbury

- *"Goodness of God"* by Bethel Music

Chapter 6

WRESTLING WITH DOUBT

Dᴇᴀʀ Younger Me,

I can remember the doubt and the questions that seemed unrelenting at night. It usually happened at night, in the quiet darkness. You often wondered if He was really there. You tried to remain faithful, but you still had to try and push those doubts down, telling yourself you shouldn't question Him and that you just needed a little more faith. But no matter how hard you tried to silence them, they remained—whispers of uncertainty that seem to get louder when life doesn't make sense.

I know how much you want to experience belief without hesitation. You desire a faith that is unshakable, unwavering, and untouched by confusion. Right now though, your faith feels fragile. You feel lost and unsure if you can fully trust the God that everyone says loves you. And I want you to know—that's okay. You see, faith was never about having all the answers. It was never about reaching a place where doubt no longer exists. Faith is about learning to trust *in the middle* of your doubts. It's about wrestling with questions, not running from them. And most of all, it's about understanding that **God is not afraid of your doubts.**

There are several questions you find hard to answer and even harder to think about. You don't want to offend God. You don't want to disappoint the people around you who seem to have their faith all figured out. But deep down, you can't shake the feeling that something isn't adding up.

- *If God is good, why did He let this happen?*

- *If He's a loving Father, why didn't He give me one?*

- *If He's with me, why does He feel so far away?*

I know how scary it is to admit that you're struggling. You don't want to seem weak. You don't want to admit that faith isn't coming as easily as you thought it would. But I need you to hear me when I say this: **Doubt doesn't mean your faith is failing. It means your faith is real.** The only people who wrestle with doubt are those who truly have faith. How can you wrestle with something that doesn't exist? After all, you have to *have* faith to doubt it, right? God knows you care about Him. If you didn't care, you wouldn't be asking these questions, and you wouldn't be fighting so hard to understand.

Some of the greatest figures in the Bible—individuals that God used in the most incredible of ways—wrestled deeply with doubt. The Disciple, Thomas, walked with Jesus, saw His miracles, and heard His teachings, yet he struggled to believe in His resurrection. Jesus didn't push Him away. Instead, He *invited* Thomas to touch His wounds, to come closer and see for himself. (John 20) King David cried out to God in frustration, questioning why He seemed too far away. (Psalm 22) And finally, my personal favorite story of Job, a man faithful to the Lord. When he was tested by the devil, Job's family died, and he lost his home and all of his possessions. He questioned the Lord, and in a whirlwind, the Lord set the record straight. When Job humbled himself, God restored almost everything taken away while he was tested twice over. (Job 42) You are not alone in doubt because everyone has doubts eventually. And God is not angry at you for it.

I used to think that doubt made God pull away from me. That if I had questions, He would tire of me and move on to someone else with stronger faith. But the opposite is actually true. God meets you in your doubt. When Thomas doubted, Jesus didn't scold him—He invited him closer. When David cried out in despair, God remained with him. When Job questioned God, God personally answered him and restored his fortunes when he humbled himself. God does not and will not abandon you because of your doubts. Instead, He invites you to wrestle through them with Him at your side.

You may feel guilty for questioning God, but let me tell you a story that changed how I see doubt. Jacob, one of the key figures in Holy Scripture, literally **wrestled with God**. He spent an entire night grappling, refusing to let go until he received a blessing. And then what happened? God *blessed* him. He didn't punish Jacob for struggling. He didn't push him away for seeking to understand. Instead, He engaged with him, allowing the struggle, and in the end, He transformed Jacob's identity—giving him a new name, Israel, meaning "he who strives with God and prevails." Your doubts, your wrestling, your questions—they are not the end of your faith. They are part of it, and God is not pushing you away; He's drawing you closer.

What I want you to know about doubt is that while you may not believe it yet, one day, you will see how God used your doubts to build something stronger in you. The questions haunting you now will lead you to a deeper understanding. The silence that frustrates you now will teach you how to listen for His voice in new ways. And those moments when you feel most abandoned will become the foundation of your testimony, a story of how God never actually left. Faith is not the absence of doubt. Faith is choosing to trust even when doubt lingers.

I know you don't have all the answers now. I know you want to believe, but sometimes it is hard. That's okay. Just keep showing up. Keep praying, even when your words and mind feel empty. Keep reading the Holy Scripture, even when the words don't immediately comfort you. Keep talking to God, even if all you can say is: "God, I don't understand." He hears you. He sees you. And He's not leaving. You may feel like you're barely holding onto God, but the truth is He is holding onto you.

With love, understanding, and unwavering hope,
Your Older Self

What happens if we don't believe something that we are expected to? What if it comes across as a little too good to be true? If you recall, I touched on the feeling of doubt in the letter to myself in the first chapter. I felt something stirring in my heart, but I wasn't sure how to address it. I didn't believe what I was feeling at first, so I ignored it. What happens to us when we feel this way? Does God get upset with us? Does He count it against us? Absolutely not, so let's talk about it. Faith and doubt often feel like opposing forces, constantly battling for control over our hearts and minds. For those of us who have grown up without a father, this battle can be intense. When the one person who was supposed to be a guiding force in our lives is absent, it's easy to question the reliability of any authority, earthly or divine.

I know what it's like to struggle in this way. I know what it's like to ask God: "God, if you love me, why did you allow this to happen?" "If You're a good father, why did You allow mine to leave me?" These questions are real, and they are bitter, but they matter. Doubt isn't something to be ashamed of; it's something to wrestle with. When we bring our doubts to God, we discover that He is not threatened by them. Instead, He meets us in the middle of them, offering reassurance, wisdom, and, most importantly, Himself. This chapter is about confronting doubt head-on, not suppressing it, not pretending it doesn't exist, but learning how to wrestle with it in a way that strengthens rather than weakens your faith.

Where does it come from? Everywhere. Just like anything on the face of this planet, everything has a beginning and comes from someplace. In the case of doubt, it comes from experiences, disappointments, unanswered questions, and confusion. For those experiencing fatherlessness, doubt often stems from the deep wound of abandonment. If an earthly father could leave, why shouldn't I expect God the Father to leave me? He's certainly capable of it, so what's stopping Him? He is. He's stopping Himself. He will not leave us nor forsake us.

Some of the most common sources of doubt are unanswered prayers, pain and suffering, contradictory experiences, and comparison. When we ask God for something and don't see the answer we expected, we wonder if He is listening. Do you think God is going to zap you with warm fuzzy feelings for some random person when you ask for love, or do you think He plays the long game and makes some lasting changes, leading you to a beautiful relationship in the future? It's definitely the long game, I promise. I've experienced it myself when I was desperate to feel loved. I felt unworthy of it, and I was almost ready to give up entirely when I met my fiancée.

When life feels upside down and is full of hardship no matter where you turn, we question why a loving God would allow it. One of the most profound movies I've ever watched is "The Shack." There is a scene in the movie where the main character, Mack, speaks with Wisdom. Mack questions why God didn't stop harm from coming to his daughter, and Wisdom's answer is that "God doesn't stop a lot of things that cause Him pain." A simple but elegant way of explaining our reality.

The earth that we live on is cursed and is not the original place we were meant to be. When Adam and Eve were exiled from the Garden of Eden, sin entered the world and, over time, created everything we experience. We live in a fallen world invaded by evil. It is the evil influences on this world that create the terrible things we see and experience. We have the audacity to blame God for it, yet humanity is the one that brought it into play. It was Eve's choice to eat of the forbidden fruit, but it was Adam's job to protect her, and both failed. This is why it is only through Christ that we are redeemed. But the curse of sin strikes again by planting seeds of doubt that cause us to stumble in our faith journey.

Contradictory experiences and comparisons to others also have a role to play in the doubt that we experience. We hear of God's blessings on others, His goodness, and His answers to prayer, but we fail to see it in our lives. We see the other families sitting at church seemingly more "blessed" than we are, and it makes our faith even harder to swallow. Why is that? Why are we subject to such an experience?

My answer is that maybe it's meant to show us something when we recognize these things. It's not to humiliate us or make us feel bad. It's just meant to highlight something in our minds because recognizing the roots of our sources of doubt is the first step in addressing them. It allows us to be honest with ourselves because if we aren't being honest with ourselves, we won't be honest with the Lord when we pray to Him. I feel like He highlights these feelings in us as a way to keep our attention to the work He is doing in our lives, even if we can't see the full picture yet.

We routinely need to remind ourselves and our friends and family that we aren't the first to suffer these trials. If you haven't done so already, you need to make it a point to read the Bible in its entirety because one of the most comforting truths about the Holy Scriptures is what I've just said. We're not the first ones to experience doubt, and God used those same people for great things. "Who are they," you may ask. Well, let's remind ourselves of these amazing figures from God's Word.

First, we have Thomas the Disciple. He is often referred to as "doubting Thomas" because he refused to believe in Jesus' resurrection until he saw physical proof. Jesus was Jesus in this moment. He didn't condemn Thomas. He loved on him, met him where he was, and provided the evidence he needed to see. In John 20:27, Jesus says to Thomas: "Put your finger here, and see my hands; and put out your hand, and place it in my side; do not be faithless, but believing." By showing His wounds, Jesus acknowledged Thomas' doubt and provided the reassurance needed for his faith to grow. If He did this for Thomas, what do you think He will do for us? Sure, our proof will be in a different form than Thomas' was, but it will be proof to us nonetheless.

Next, we have Gideon. When God called on Gideon to be a mighty warrior, he questioned whether God had abandoned Israel and asked for multiple signs to confirm his calling. Finally, Gideon received confirmation from an Angel of God and went into battle, striking the Midianites and delivering Israel's victory.

The Psalms are filled with moments where David questions God's presence and struggles with fear, only to reaffirm his trust in the end. This feels similar to what I feel. I have peaks and valleys in my faith walk with Jesus, and in those valleys, I struggle. In those moments, not only do I doubt, but I doubt that I'm saved because of my doubt. It's not until I am reminded that doubt is only a minor setback used to distract us from the truth.

Finally, we have John the Baptist. In Matthew 3, John baptizes Jesus, but later in Matthew 11:2-6 sends his messengers to Jesus asking Him: "Are you He who is to come, or shall we look for another?" When Jesus sends word back to John, He says, "Go and tell John what you hear and see: the blind receive their sight and the lame walk, lepers are cleansed, and the deaf hear, and the dead are raised up, and the poor have good news preached to them. And blessed is he who takes no offense at me."

Even the men whom we know now had the greatest examples of faith had doubt in their journey. So, if these great men had moments of doubt, then it's okay for us to have them too. The key is what they did in their doubts; they brought them to God instead of letting the doubts drive them away from faith in Him. So, when doubts creep into your mind, immediately seek community. A trusted brother or sister in Christ or your pastor so that you can be properly guided.

Doubt itself clearly isn't the problem, as we've just explored. It's when doubt festers and remains unresolved that it becomes dangerous. Unchecked doubt can lead to spiritual paralysis, bitterness, and drifting away from our faith. When we stop praying, reading the Bible, or going to Church, we stop seeking God because we don't know if it's worth it. The bitterness that begins to set in turns into resentment because it makes it difficult for us to see the goodness God is pouring into our lives. We refuse to believe in miracles when they happen around us every day, though we are unaware. When this doubt and bitterness goes unaddressed, it creates distance between us and God, making it easier to walk away altogether. So, this is why we must wrestle with doubt rather than ignore it. Doubt should be a doorway to deeper faith, not an excuse to walk away.

If doubt is part of the journey, then how are we supposed to engage with it in a healthy way? In what ways can we engage in a way that strengthens our relationship with God rather than weakens it? I have a few answers for this, so let's look at them one at a time:

1. Bring Your Doubts to God

He already knows what you're struggling with. Instead of attempting to hide it, talk with Him honestly about it. Pray like David did in the Psalms: "How long, O Lord? Will you forget me forever? How long will you hide your face from me?" (Psalm 13:1) God is big and strong enough to handle your hardest questions, so give Him the opportunity.

2. Seek Answers, Not Excuses

Some doubts exist because we haven't searched for the answers. Read Scripture, study theology, and seek wise counsel. Don't let a lack of knowledge and understanding become a reason to walk away. It is okay to ask questions.

3. Remember Past Faithfulness

When doubt clouds your vision, look back on times when God was faithful to you. Does your present momentary doubt render past faithfulness moot? Absolutely not! Remind yourself of these moments, and keep a journal of answered prayers and those moments when you've felt His presence.

4. Surround Yourself with People Who Strengthen Your Faith

Prior to giving our lives to the Lord, we've all lived lives and been around people and situations we probably shouldn't have. Does that mean you drop everyone and everything like a lead brick? Maybe, depending on what it is, but it's also important to share your faith with your past. Maybe you can help the Lord plant seeds in the hearts of those who need it the most. Additionally, doubt thrives in isolation. Talking to other believers, especially those who have wrestled with similar doubts, can provide encouragement and perspective.

5. Take Action Despite Doubt

Faith isn't the absence of doubt. It's choosing to trust God even when doubts exist. Sometimes, the best way to overcome doubt is to keep moving forward in faith, even when you don't feel like it.

For many of us, doubt is not a one-time experience. It's something we revisit throughout our lives. There will be seasons where faith comes easily, and there will be seasons where every prayer feels unanswered. But doubt doesn't disqualify you from God's love, nor does it mean your faith is weak. This was especially true for me to understand. When I felt this way, I felt that my faith was weak and not strong enough to overcome even the simplest of obstacles.

I used to think that struggling with doubt meant that I wasn't a good Christian. But now I see that wrestling with doubt is part of what makes faith real. It's in the struggle that I have learned to rely on God, to seek Him more intentionally, and to trust Him even when I don't have all the answers. After all, much like physical exercise, you don't see improvement unless you work on it over time. If you're in a season of doubt, I want you to know this: God is still with you. He's not angry at you for questioning. He's drawing you closer through it. Keep seeking Him. Keep asking. Keep wrestling. Because, in the end, faith isn't about having every answer. It's about trusting the One who does.

Doubt is not the enemy of faith; it is an opportunity for deeper trust. When we bring our doubts to God, we give Him the chance to reveal Himself in new and powerful ways. So don't run from your questions. Wrestle with them, bring them before God, and let them lead you to a faith that is even stronger than before.

Reflection Questions

1. What doubts have you struggled with in your faith journey?

2. How have you seen God's faithfulness in the past, even in difficult seasons?

3. What steps can you take today to wrestle with doubt in a healthy way?

Devotional Thought

"I believe; help my unbelief!" — Mark 9:24

Even in doubt, we can cry out to God, trusting that He will meet us where we are.

Recommended Reading

- *"The Case for Faith"* by Lee Strobel

- *"Faith & Doubt"* by John Ortberg

- *"Disappointment with God"* by Philip Yancey

Recommended Songs

- *"Even If"* by MercyMe

- *"Oceans (Where Feet May Fail)"* by Hillsong United

- *"Way Maker"* by Leeland

Chapter 7

THE ROLE OF FATHER FIGURES

H EY Me,
It's time we directly address the vacancy in your life and talk about some of those individuals who helped you along the way. I know how much you've longed for someone to step into the role that Dad left empty. It's an ache you don't talk about often, but it's there. A quiet wish for guidance, protection, and someone to say that they're proud of you. Mom was all of these things. I know you won't forget that, But, sometimes you want it to come from a different source. I know how hard you tried to pretend that it didn't matter. The times you would brush it off as if not having a father in your life was no big deal. But it is. That longing you've felt all these years, the one that whispers: "I wish someone would see me, teach me, care for me," is valid.

What you may not realize right now is that God places people in our lives who step into that role momentarily, even if they may not carry the title of "Dad" or "Step-Dad." These people can be coaches, teachers, pastors, mentors, neighbors, and friends. Placing these important people in your life is God's way of providing the guidance and love you've been missing. They are not perfect, but their influence is real, and it matters.

I wish I could tell you to appreciate them more than you will while they are in your life. There will be moments when their words or actions will leave an imprint on your heart, even if you don't realize it at the time. That teacher who believed in you and could see your bigger potential even when you doubted yourself and couldn't see it. Your friend's father who welcomed you into his home and treated you like one of his own? They're all part of the tapestry God is weaving to help you grow.

But I also know this truth: the presence of these figures won't fully erase the ache of not having your father around. And that's okay. It's not their job to replace what was lost. It's their job to show up and offer what they can. Your job is to recognize their gifts, to be grateful for the guidance they give, and to allow yourself to learn from them. I remember times when you resisted the influence of these figures because you didn't want to seem like you needed help. You thought leaning on someone else was a sign of weakness, but it's not. Allowing people to step into your life and guide you is a sign of strength, wisdom, and trust.

What you'll realize in time is that God, in His infinite love, works through imperfect people. God has a way of using the least likely candidates. They are a reflection of His heart for you, a heart that wants to protect, guide, and affirm you in ways you might not fully understand yet. Even when your earthly father couldn't be there, your Heavenly Father has always been present, orchestrating relationships that could provide what you needed.

You'll also learn that father figures aren't just there to teach you; they're there to challenge you. Some of the lessons will be hard, and some will sting, but those moments will shape you. The discipline you hated at the moment will later become the wisdom you live by. The advice you shrug off will become the principles you pass down to others. You may not fully appreciate the role of father figures in your life until later when you look back and see the threads of influence they wove into your story. But when you do, I hope you'll see them for what they are: gifts from God.

One day, you'll have the chance to be a father figure to someone else. Maybe it will be your own children, or maybe it will be a young person who looks up to you the way you looked up to others. When that time comes, you'll understand how much courage, effort, and love it takes to step into that role. And when you do, I hope you'll remember how much those figures meant to you, even when you didn't know how to say it.

So, younger me, lean into these relationships. Be open to their wisdom, even when it challenges you. Be grateful for their presence, even when it feels imperfect. And most importantly, remember that through them,

God is showing you a glimpse of His fatherly love, a love that will never fail you, no matter what.

With gratitude and love,
Your Older Self

Not all fathers are biological. Sometimes, God places people in our lives who step into that role. They can be mentors, teachers, coaches, pastors, the parents of your friends, and so many other things. These individuals may not carry the title of "Dad," but their presence and guidance can shape us in profound ways. For someone like me, who grew up without a father, these figures became a patchwork quilt of wisdom, support, and love, and they were essential to my upbringing.

While they couldn't fully fill the void left by my father's absence, their influence mattered. They taught me lessons I didn't know I needed, challenged me in ways I resisted, and gave me glimpses of what healthy fatherhood could look like. This chapter explores the impact these relationships can have, how to recognize their value, and how God uses them as reflections of His own fatherly love.

Fatherlessness leaves an undeniable mark, one that often manifests as a longing for guidance, protection, and affirmation. It's not just an absence. It's a void, a question that lingers in the back of your mind: "Why wasn't I enough for him to stay?" As a child, I didn't fully understand the weight of that void. I didn't have the words to articulate what I was missing, but I felt it. It wasn't until I saw the interactions my friends had with their fathers that I began to realize what I was missing.

Seemingly unimportant experiences and lessons like throwing a football to achieve that perfect spiral, which I still can't do to this day...Helping you with your homework, showing up to school or sports events, or simply saying, "I'm proud of you." I would watch from the sidelines, pretending it didn't bother me, but deep down, I wished someone would do the same for me. The absence of a father creates a hunger for someone to step into that role, even if it's not consciously acknowledged. That hunger often leads us to seek father figures, sometimes without even realizing it. This void isn't just emotional. It's practical too. Fathers are often the ones who teach their children skills, from tying a tie to changing tires. Without that guidance, you're left to figure it out on your own. While independence can be a strength, it often comes with a sense of isolation.

For me, that isolation was a lack of knowing where to start. I would get so lost in the details of a project that I would psych myself out from the start, and I still do this to this day. Household chores that seem simple to my friends seem nearly impossible for me to accomplish because I'm left unable to wrap my head around it. Or, I will get knee deep into a seemingly easy project only to be stumped by something I didn't expect. I would have to call someone in to help me fix the problem. It was embarrassing to me that I was left with this need to constantly rely on people to fix these problems as if I'm not able to handle my own household. It is a deeply scarring feeling not being able to be a "man's man," that is, not being able to handle the stereotypical expectations of you.

Thankfully, God didn't leave me there, alone in that void. Throughout my life, He placed a series of father figures in my path, each contributing something unique. What is important here is that you are not fooled by who these people can be. I mentioned specific roles they could be, but I want to give special notice that I never said it had to be a man. At my youngest, one of the most formative women in my life was "Grandma Marion," my preschool teacher. She taught me how to play "Twinkle, Twinkle Little Star" on the piano. She guided my mother in ways I'll never have the privilege to know and remained in my life until she passed away. Grandma Marion was the sweetest of souls, and I look forward to the day when I can reunite with her again in God's presence.

I've had several teachers who saw potential in me that I couldn't see in myself. School was not a joyful place for me. I was not comfortable there whatsoever. I did the bare minimum to pass, and I graduated high school with a 2.1 GPA. These teachers told me that I was capable of much more than I realized, and those lessons stayed with me, challenging me to dream bigger.

I've had several pastors in my life as well who not only taught me more about God but modeled the way fathers were meant to lead their families. Their guidance helped me see that a relationship with God could be personal and real. It was possible to move past the brick wall obstructing my path and to be the person that God wanted me to be. He wasn't going to let something like this keep me from achieving my potential.

And then there was John. The father of my friend Mike, whom I'm still friends with. I met Mike while in kindergarten, and that was that. We got along instantly and are best friends to this day. Mike's dad welcomed me into his home like one of his own. In many ways, it felt like he adopted me because of how close Mike and I were to each other. And yes, I had refrigerator privileges while I was at their house. He didn't have to, but John expressed his generosity and kindness in ways that made me feel seen and valued in ways I never experienced elsewhere.

Each of these individuals offered pieces of what I needed: guidance, encouragement, discipline, and love. Together, they formed a patchwork quilt of influence stitched together by God Himself. Nothing short of a miracle. God was able to do this with the people I least expected Him to. The impact will last through the rest of my life and well into the next generation now that I am a father myself.

The experience of being taught lessons that go beyond words is life-changing. One experience of mine in particular taught me that discipline builds strength. I was a member of the United States Naval Sea Cadet Corps, a great program for kids aged 10-18 who are interested in learning about the military without actually having to join after the program. I highly recommend it, not only because I still participate in this program as an adult volunteer on occasion but also because it taught me the discipline I needed at a young age. Discipline that you would normally expect a father to impart to his children.

Excellence was demanded, and mediocrity was forbidden. Perfection was never expected, nor was the goal, but doing the best you can in the situation you're given was the overarching lesson. At the time, I thought it was unfair and often too strict, but looking back, I see how much it made me care about myself and those around me. The uniform inspections instilled in me pride in how I look and devotion to the idea that the uniform I was wearing was worn by men and women who made the ultimate sacrifice. The discipline I was learning was never about making my life difficult. It was about helping me become stronger, both mentally and physically.

I've mentioned before that while growing up, school wasn't a favorite thing in my life, especially math. Math was a major struggle for me, and it wasn't until college that I had a professor help me figure something out. In doing so, she also poured into me some self-esteem. She told me that I was much smarter than I was giving myself credit for. You see, my issue in math is that I cannot recall the process of solving problems. It was her that recognized the symptoms and asked me for clarification. I told her that I routinely forgot the process of solving problems. I would get to a question on a test and do part of the work, only to move on to the next question because I didn't remember the next steps.

She told me that with what she saw, I should see a specialist for diagnosis of dyscalculia, essentially the math form of dyslexia. Characterized by memory loss specific to math, the reversal of symbols and numbers in an equation, and difficulty doing things in your head like counting back change, calculating tips, or estimating a sale price on an item at the store. Once she gave me the thought that it wasn't my fault and that it was something I just had to work through, I was able to pass her class easily. Over time, I began to believe that she was right and that maybe I was capable of more than I thought.

Not all father figures express love through words. This is crucial to understand and grasp. As a father and stepfather, I find expressing myself in spoken words incredibly difficult at times. I am able to express myself more easily in written form. I know what you're thinking: "No kidding, as I'm reading your book!" All jokes aside, many father figures show love in other ways, such as through action. Showing up to an important event, seeing difficulty and giving advice, or simply being present and wanting to spend time with you. Each of these are equally valid ways to express affection, and it was difficult for me to understand that at first. It is important for you to understand that each person on this earth is different, and they each have the right to be respected regardless of the way they express themselves. It took a while for me to recognize these things as acts of love, even when they didn't look like what I thought a father's love should be.

If I'm an expert in anything, it's making mistakes. I'm not talking about the little things, either. I'm talking about life-changing things. I had an experience with someone that hurt quite a bit, but when we went our separate ways, she left with some advice. That despite my mistakes, they are part of the journey. It was her belief that mistakes happen but that they are part of the tapestry God is sowing. Her opinion was that God allowed certain things to happen because it allowed the ultimate destination of His plan to take place.

While father figures bring guidance and support, their influence isn't always perfect. They are human, after all, and their imperfections can sometimes lead to disappointment. There were plenty of times when I placed unrealistic expectations on a father figure. I hoped that they would fill the void my father left vacant, but they were unable to. I held resentment for some of these father figures because of this, and they had no idea that I held them to this standard. It wasn't fair of me to do this, especially since they weren't even aware I had done this. It was mostly a subconscious thought, but nonetheless, the expectation was there. This hurt because it stood as a constant reminder of what I had lost and what I didn't have.

Yet other father figures in my life let me down in other ways, those who didn't follow through. I had teachers and family members overlook my potential and who weren't emotionally available as I had hoped. Those moments were painful, but they taught an important lesson: Father figures aren't replacements. They're supplements. Their roles are not to erase the pain of an absent father but to offer what they can with what they have. It is not impossible to have the greatest experience with a father figure. I've seen plenty of YouTube videos where stepchildren ask their stepfathers to adopt them. That is an example of a father figure who stepped in and healed in inexplicable ways. I would love nothing more than to have that confirmation that throughout my presence and influence, despite my faults and mistakes, my heart shined through.

The influence of father figures is a gift, not meant to fully fill the void left by an absent father. That is filled by God's grace and love. The ones He places in our lives are meant to teach us, guide us, and remind us that we are loved and we are never alone. Their presence is a reflection of God's love and care, showing us glimpses of the perfect Father we have in Him.

As we move into the next chapter, take time to reflect on the father figures in your life: the mentors, teachers, pastors, and friends who have shaped who you are. Appreciate their impact, regardless of the lack of perfection. If there was a falling out of some sort, if it is appropriate, reach out to remind that person how important they were to you. If you feel called like I did, step into this role for someone else. We have an astounding epidemic of fatherless homes in this country. Volunteer your time with the Boys and Girls Club of America, Meals on Wheels, a foster care setting, or a children's hospital, for example. You may never fully understand the impact and difference you'd make in the life of someone else but trust that God will use you to be part of His patchwork quilt in someone else's life. All you have to do is speak with God, ask Him where He needs you, and say to Him: "Here am I. Send me."

Reflection Questions

1. Who have been the father figures in your life, and what lessons did they teach you?

2. How have you seen God's love reflected through these relationships?

3. In what ways can you be a father figure to someone else?

Devotional Thought

"A father to the fatherless, a defender of widows, is God in his holy dwelling." — Psalm 68:5

Reflect on how God has used father figures in your life to reveal His love and care.

Recommended Reading

- *"The Mentor Leader"* by Tony Dungy

- *"Father Fiction"* by Donald Miller

- *"Wild at Heart"* by John Eldredge

Recommended Songs

- *"Good Good Father"* by Chris Tomlin

- *"I Love You This Much"* by Jimmy Wayne

- *"You Say"* by Lauren Daigle

Chapter 8

FINDING PURPOSE AND DIRECTION

D<small>EAR</small> Me,
   It's overwhelming, isn't it? You're at the intersection of uncertainty and motivation, curious about which direction will lead you to a meaningful purpose and fulfillment. You have a motivated side that wants to conquer the world, but you have no clue *what* you are called to do. On the one hand, you don't want to unnecessarily waste time by going in the wrong direction, but on the other, you know you have to start somewhere. What makes this part the hardest is that you have no starting point, no foundation of personal interests, or desires of knowledge in a particular subject matter. As you always seem to do, you begin asking questions. "Why am I here?" "Does life really matter?" "What does God want from me?"

   At this point in life, you feel directionless. You drift from moment to moment, desperate for clarity, but you have no clue how to find it. Remember, I was there with you because I am you. We walked those paths together, feeling just as lost, just as uncertain, and just desperate to discover our purpose. You might not fully understand this yet, but your questions are evidence of something beautiful and powerful within you. They are proof that God is stirring your heart. He created you with a purpose—a unique, deeply personal, and God-designed purpose that no one else can fulfill in the same way. I can make you this promise right now: That despite feeling lost, every step you've taken, even the ones that felt more like a stumble, has brought you closer to discovering what you were uniquely created to do.

Remember the words of Jeremiah 29:11: "For I know the plans I have for you," says the Lord, "plans for welfare and not for evil, to give you a future and hope." I know it feels hard to trust those words right now, especially because you grew up without a constant in your life. Where most other kids your age grew up with their fathers leading them and guiding their paths, you didn't experience the same thing. Without a clear voice of encouragement and direction, you sometimes feel left to navigate this complicated world alone. I need you to hear me and listen to me clearly right now because it is vitally important. You have *never* been alone. God has always been walking with you, even through your confusion. He was leading and guiding you this entire time, even when everything seemed loud and overwhelming. His quiet, gentle nature shined through on your path, serving as the lighthouse you needed to find your way.

The world often paints purpose as something distant. A seemingly grand revelation or epiphany one experiences at some random point in their life, supposedly at the peak of your greatest achievements. One day, the lightbulb just illuminates, and all of your problems go away. This couldn't be further from the truth. It is important to note that having a purpose heavily influences your identity. We already spoke about the search for identity, but take this moment as a reminder of that lesson since the two are linked.

The truth that I discovered—and the truth that I desperately wish you grasp—is that purpose is often revealed in small, everyday steps of obedience and trust. Purpose doesn't come wrapped neatly with a ribbon, announced in a single moment of divine clarity. Rather, it unfolds gradually as you walk faithfully through life's joys and struggles, always trusting that your Creator has the greater picture in mind. Let me remind you of a verse that has guided my journey, especially when the path seemed hidden: Proverbs 3:5-6; "Trust in the Lord with all your heart and do not rely on your own insight. In all your ways acknowledge Him, and He will make straight your paths." Notice the simplicity and depth of this promise. God is not asking you to have everything figured out. He isn't expecting perfection or that you'll never misstep. Instead, He simply calls you to trust, to acknowledge His presence in each decision, large or small. When you do this consistently, clarity comes—not always immediately—but always in His perfect timing.

You will encounter seasons of waiting, moments when it feels as though God has placed your purpose on hold. Don't despise these moments; embrace them. Waiting seasons are sacred spaces. They are training grounds where patience, character, and resilience grow. It's in these moments that your relationship with God will deepen profoundly. You will learn to rely less on what you can see and more on the certainty of who God is.

Consider the story of Joseph in Genesis. Joseph's life was filled with setbacks, betrayals, and years of painful waiting. He was abandoned by his brothers, unjustly imprisoned, and seemingly forgotten. Yet, through each trial, Joseph remained faithful. He experienced many emotions during this time, and that is okay. It's okay to be angry and sad in the midst of the trial. Eventually, God raised him into a position where his purpose became clear—saving not only Egypt but also the very family who betrayed him. (Genesis 50:20) Joseph's story teaches us something powerful: even our pain has a purpose. Even the years we deem wasted are actively preparing us for what lies ahead.

I know the ache in your heart—the longing to understand exactly what God has in store for you. But consider this: what if God's greatest desire isn't just to reveal your purpose but rather for you to trust Him deeply enough that you would follow Him anywhere, even before your purpose unfolds? Take comfort in Ephesians 2:10, which says, "For we are his workmanship, created in Christ Jesus for good works, which God prepared beforehand, that we should walk in them." You are not an accident. Your dreams, your passions, your unique talents—they're not random! They were thoughtfully woven into your life's tapestry by the God who knows you better than you know yourself. Trust Him with your story. Every experience you've had—even growing up without your father—has shaped you in ways that uniquely qualify you to help others find hope, healing, and direction in Christ. You will soon discover that your purpose isn't confined to one role, job title, or accomplishment. Your true purpose is deeper: it's about bringing glory to God through everything you do. Whether through your career, your relationships, your passions, or even your struggles, your life's purpose is ultimately to reflect the beauty and faithfulness of God.

I think about your sister and brother, Tiffany and Joshua, and the different journeys they've taken. Tiffany, motivated by compassion and a desire to break down barriers, began her career as a sign language interpreter in public schools. She used her hands and heart to connect people who might otherwise have lived an isolated, misunderstood life, cut off from the rest of the world due to the simple inability to communicate. Her career was not something she happened upon; it was a calling that God placed in her heart, fueled by her empathy and desire to serve others meaningfully. She has blessed so many lives in her career, and I am so proud of her. Her career continues now in public school administration, and I know that she will continue to serve others in her new role.

Then there is Joshua, or Joshy, as you've known him your whole life. He is a brave and determined soul, beginning his career by stepping into the fire service as a paid-on-call firefighter and EMT. His journey toward purpose has led him to risk his life for others, fighting to protect, preserve, and save lives, homes, and communities. His path, though different, is equally powerful. It is his courage that shaped his purpose, serving as a reflection of God's heart for rescue, restoration, and selfless love. Joshy continues his career as head of security for a public school district in North Dakota. I'm so proud of him as well, and all that he has endured to get where he is today.

Their paths illustrate an essential truth: God's purpose for each person is beautifully unique. It's not limited to ministry positions or overtly spiritual roles. God's calling spans countless paths, including everyday roles that touch the lives of so many in profound ways. Both of my siblings found their purpose through a combination of listening to the inner voice God placed within them and bravely stepping forward, even when the future was uncertain. When God called, they answered "Here am I. Send me." (Isaiah 6:8)

Don't waste your time comparing your path to the paths of others. Your journey isn't supposed to look like theirs. It is meant to stand out from all the others. God doesn't measure by the world's standards; He measures by faithfulness, obedience, and love. Remember Proverbs 19:21

here, "Many are the plans in the mind of a man, but it is the purpose of the Lord that will be established." Trust the process, trust your story, and most importantly, trust the One who's writing it.

Today, you may only see fragments, disconnected pieces of your life. But God sees the entire masterpiece. Keep stepping forward. Keep praying. Keep seeking wisdom. Each step, even when uncertain, brings you closer to the life God has beautifully planned for you. Purpose is found not only in your strengths and victories but also in your weaknesses and struggles. As Paul wrote in 2 Corinthians 12:9, "My grace is sufficient for you, for my power is made perfect in weakness." Even on the hardest days, God is preparing you to show the world how beautiful and powerful God's grace truly is.

Take heart because your purpose is unfolding beautifully—even in moments when it feels obscured by uncertainty. God will lead you exactly where you need to go. I believe in you, not because I know all that you'll achieve, but because I know the One who is guiding you. I know the faithfulness of the God who will never let you down. You can trust His plan, even when you cannot fully see it. Your future is filled with meaning, purpose, and joy—because it is full of Him.

With profound hope, love, and clarity from the future,
Your Older Self

At some point during our lives, we all stand face-to-face with the profound question: "*Why am I here?*" For those who have grown into adolescence or adulthood without a father's guiding voice, this question is loud. It presses harder on our minds, and is significantly harder to answer. Without a clear roadmap or someone who models purposeful living, the search for direction can become overwhelming. Yet, this journey, while challenging, can also become deeply transformative when we allow God to lead the way.

I spent many years wandering through life, feeling as though everyone else around me had uncovered their calling, while I struggled to find even the smallest hint of mine. My questions echoed louder in the silence, especially when watching others confidently pursue careers, relationships, and passions. But looking back on it now, I realize that those moments of uncertainty weren't a waste—they were essential parts of my path to discovering purpose and direction. In this chapter, I want to share with you how that journey unfolded, the truths God revealed to me, and how you can discover the profound purpose He has woven uniquely into your life's tapestry.

For a long time, I believed that purpose was something elusive—something only a fortunate few stumbled upon and had the chance to experience. I saw it as a singular, life-defining moment, wrapped neatly in success, recognition, or a clear-cut calling. However, God slowly reshaped my understanding. Purpose, I discovered, is not a destination; it's a journey of obedience, trust, and a daily commitment to surrender to God's plan for your life.

Ephesians 2:10 reminds us clearly, "For we are God's handiwork, created in Christ Jesus to do good works, which God prepared in advance for us to do." You are uniquely crafted by God, intentionally designed for good works ahead of time. Your purpose isn't limited to a specific job, title, or role—it's found in consistently glorifying God, whenever you are and whatever you're doing. One of the greatest revelations in my journey came when I learned that purpose wasn't about achieving one singular goal or task. Instead, it is the ongoing discovery of how God wants to use you right where you are—in your family, your friendships, your career, your community, and even your challenges.

Growing up without a father's presence left gaps—gaps in guidance, affirmation, and clarity. It felt like everyone else had a built-in navigator while I was a sailboat left to drift in the currents of the ocean. The absence of an earthly father made trusting a Heavenly Father challenging, especially in something as personal as purpose. This is true even today, in the version of you that is writing these words. But God began gently revealing that He had always been guiding me, even when I didn't see it, or worse, when I refused to see it. Psalm 32:8 became an anchor for me during these uncertain times: "I will instruct you and teach you in the way you should go; I will counsel you with my loving eye on you." So, though my earthly father was absent, my Heavenly Father was always present. He was guiding my steps even in confusion. I realized that my lack of earthly direction wasn't a limitation on my life. It was an invitation to rely entirely on God. He became my ultimate source of clarity, affirmation, and wisdom.

One of the most challenging yet beautiful lessons in finding purpose is learning to trust God's timing. We live in a culture that demands immediate answers, but God often moves slowly, intentionally shaping our character through waiting. Waiting isn't passive; it's profoundly active. It's in these periods of waiting that we learn to lean on God's promises rather than our understanding. Isaiah 40:31 offers powerful assurance: "But those who wait upon the Lord shall renew their strength; they shall mount up with wings like eagles, they shall run and not be weary, they shall walk and not grow faint." Waiting became my training ground for deeper faith, teaching me patience, trust, and reliance on God. It was in these quiet, seemingly directionless seasons that God developed the resilience and faith I would later need to walk confidently in my purpose.

Discovering your purpose involves identifying the gifts and passions God has placed within you. Romans 12:6 says: "We have different gifts, according to the grace given to each of us." Your gifts aren't accidental —they're clues to how God intends to use you. I recall how clearly I saw this unfold with my sister and brother, Tiffany and Joshua. Tiffany followed her passion for helping people communicate and connect, becoming a sign language interpreter. Her unique blend of compassion, patience, and diligence revealed a clear picture of purpose—serving as a bridge for those who might otherwise have lived a life in silence. In contrast, Joshua stepped boldly into a career of firefighting, no doubt by watching his father and grandfather do the same. It is a life driven by bravery, a deep sense of justice, and a desire to protect others. His calling emerged naturally from his gifts of courage and resilience, showing me another powerful example of God's purposeful design in each of us. Witnessing their journeys taught me that my purpose might look completely different from theirs—and that was perfectly okay. It freed me to embrace my own path, to blaze my own trail without the poison of comparison or self-doubt.

Another lesson that was hard to learn that pain carries a hidden purpose. My father's absence, the wounds I've endured and struggle to heal, the struggles I face in general—they're not random or meaningless. God redeems all pain and transforms it into purpose. Joseph's story in Genesis is a powerful example. Betrayed, imprisoned, and forgotten, Joseph endured tremendous pain. Yet in the end, he recognized that what others intended for harm, God intended for good. I've met many people along my journey who struggle in their relationship with God because of a certain event or obstacle in their life that was outside their control, yet, deeply wounded their hearts. They had a hard time trusting that God wasn't behind the tragedy. A wonderful and insightful line in the movie "The Shack" works in well here: "I [God] can work incredible good out of unspeakable tragedies, but that doesn't mean I orchestrate the tragedies." Your struggles are similarly being redeemed, shaping you to help others experiencing similar hurt. I've seen God transform my fatherlessness into compassion for others who feel abandoned. He has turned my questions and doubts into a ministry of encouragement. Your pain, your story, will become a powerful testimony of God's redemption.

In my search for purpose and direction, I encountered a strong and often difficult emotion: anger. Anger towards my dad, anger at God for allowing me to feel abandoned, and anger at myself for struggling to figure things out. At first, I didn't understand how anger related to my purpose, but I came to see that it played a significant role. Unresolved anger clouds our vision, and it keeps us trapped in bitterness. It distracts us from seeing the beauty that God has laid out ahead of us. Ephesians 4:26 provides powerful wisdom: "In your anger do not sin: Do not let the sun go down while you are still angry."

Anger by itself isn't wrong or sinful—it is a natural human emotion. There is a such thing as righteous anger, and we see an example of this when Jesus flips the tables in the Temple Courts of Jerusalem. You can read about it in the Gospels of Matthew 21, Mark 11, and Luke 19. It is what we do with our anger that matters. If we allow it to fester, it becomes bitterness, preventing us from fully embracing our God-given purpose. But if we confront our anger openly with God, we create space for healing and clarity.

In my own journey, acknowledging my anger allowed me to process the deeper wounds that caused it. I recognized that beneath my anger was grief—grief over what I'd missed out on, grief over lost opportunities, and grief over unmet expectations. By bringing this grief honestly before God, my anger transformed from a barrier into a stepping stone. God used it to reveal deeper insights about forgiveness, compassion, and patience.

If you're wrestling with anger, I encourage you to face it openly rather than suppress it. Talk to God honestly about your feelings, even if they are uncomfortable or messy. He can handle your raw emotion. Ask Him to reveal the roots of your anger and to heal those deep wounds, allowing you to move forward freely toward your purpose. Remember, your anger doesn't have to define you. Instead, it can refine you, making you more compassionate, understanding, and prepared for the calling God has placed on your life. Finding purpose doesn't have to be abstract. Here are some practical steps you can take:

1. **Seek God in Prayer** — Purpose is often revealed through an intimacy with God. You need to commit to spending time daily in His presence. Have a conversation with Him as often as possible, asking for guidance and clarity.

2. **Explore Your Passions and Gifts** — Pay close attention to activities that make you feel alive. Your purpose often aligns with your natural talents and interests.

3. **Serve Others** — Often, purpose is found when we shift our focus away from ourselves into an outwardly direction. Serving others clarifies what matters most.

4. **Seek Wise Counsel** — Allow trusted mentors and friends to speak into your life, myself included. If you've read this far, I hope that I've been helpful to you and that you've come to trust my words. God often uses the people we surround ourselves with to reveal our strengths and direction.

Discovering purpose is not a one-time event; it's a lifelong pursuit of trusting God, seeking His guidance, and obediently following where He leads. You may not have every answer now, but remember—purpose unfolds one step of faithfulness at a time. God created you with intention, and your life holds unfathomable meaning beyond your wildest imaginations. Trust Him. Walk forward, even if you cannot see the path forward. Those faithful steps that you take could change everything. Your story is still unfolding, and your purpose is greater than you know.

Reflection Questions

1. What activities make you feel most alive and connected with God?

2. How have past experiences shaped your passions and strengths?

3. What steps can you take this week to pursue clarity in your purpose?

Devotional Thought

"Trust in the Lord with all your heart, and do not rely on your own insight. In all your ways acknowledge Him, and He will make straight your paths." -Proverbs 3:5-6

Recommended Resources

- *The Purpose Driven Life* by Rick Warren

- *Garden City: Work, Rest, and the Art of Being Human* by John Mark Comer

- *Let Your Life Speak* by Parker Palmer

Music

- *"You Say"* by Lauren Daigle

- *"Oceans (Where Feet May Fail)"* by Hillsong United

Chapter 9

OVERCOMING ANGER AND BITTERNESS

H EY Younger Me,
    That's some heavy weight you're carrying, almost too heavy. You can't lie to me, Brenton, I'm you, and I know what you're thinking. You walk through life trying to hide it, trying to act as if the anger and bitterness aren't quietly shaping your thoughts, decisions, and relationships. You have become so jaded, so skilled at masking the pain beneath the surface, that you can force a smile or an indifferent shrug that sometimes even fools yourself into thinking that you've moved on. Guess what? You haven't, so stop lying to yourself. When everything goes quiet, when you're alone, the truth is undeniable because the anger and bitterness are still there, buried deep, unresolved, and powerful.

Please don't shut down on me, because you have every reason to feel this way, to feel hurt. Growing up without your father around created the deepest wound, deeper than most people could ever understand. It's not about the absence—it's about the deep pain of what could have been; the memories never created, conversations imagined but never actually spoken, affirmations never heard. The anger you feel often arises from these unmet expectations. It is the lingering sense of injustice that someone who should have loved you unconditionally simply chose not to be there.

I can remember that burning anger in our belly, it's a feeling that I'll never forget because it was mine for so long. I felt it deeply, day after day, silently blaming my father for every misstep, every struggle, every insecurity, and every embarrassment. Sometimes I directed that anger inward, believing that I wasn't enough—that perhaps his absence meant that something was inherently wrong with me. Other times, I turned that anger outward, resentful at others who had what I didn't, and bitter toward people who didn't even realize they triggered my pain. The resentment felt justified, a shield protecting me from being hurt again. Yet, deep down, it never protected me at all; it only isolated me even further into the darkness.

You might believe that holding onto anger somehow keeps you strong. Let me assure you of how wrong you are; anger and bitterness don't strengthen—they weaken, slowly stealing the joy that God intended for your life. Remember what I said earlier about the goals of the devil? The devil only comes to steal, kill, and destroy anything that has God's favor, including the joy that you could feel despite your situation. Anger and bitterness can blind us to the good things right in front of our faces, creating walls that even love struggles to climb. They can distort our perception of who God is, making it difficult to trust in His goodness and love.

I have so many profound lessons to share amongst these letters, and so here is another one. Your anger? It's not wrong. It's understandable. It's human. Even Jesus experienced anger when confronted with injustice and harm. But holding onto it and allowing it to settle into bitterness is where the trouble lies. Ephesians 4:26-27: "Be angry but do not sin; do not let the sun go down on your anger, and give no opportunity to the devil." This passage doesn't shame us for feeling angry; rather, it lovingly warns us about the danger of letting anger fester, allowing it to settle in our hearts where it gives darkness a foothold.

Brenton, please, it's okay to admit that you're hurting. It's okay to admit that you feel abandoned, even angry. But today, I'm gently asking you to please consider that staying angry is a choice. Choosing to remain bitter only prolongs your pain. It keeps you chained to the very thing you want so desperately to be free from.

I used to believe that forgiveness was something people talked about but rarely practiced. Forgiving felt like defeat, like surrendering my pain as if it never mattered. It felt like I was letting my father off the hook for him to never face the consequences of what his decisions meant for me and my life. But over time, God patiently taught me that forgiveness doesn't dismiss the hurt; it frees the heart. Forgiveness releases the weight of bitterness. It removes the chains that have bound your joy and kept you locked in that prison of resentment. God also revealed to my eyes that forgiveness is an act of courage, and it is one of the bravest steps that you will ever take.

I learned this lesson one night after years of silently carrying this heavy weight around my neck. I sat quietly in prayer, exhausted by the heavy load. It was then that I finally voiced my pain aloud, confronting the deepest hurts—the unmet needs, the abandonment, the unfairness, the injustice. In that quiet place, the Holy Spirit made His presence well known. He was there with me, just as He'd always been, but this time in this sacred space, God met me with His immeasurable power on display for me to witness. He didn't shame me for my anger and bitterness; instead, I felt His presence gently invite me to trust Him with it. In my mind, I imagined Him kneeling before me, gesturing to take it from me, and I let Him do just that. In this place, it felt like I was having my own "burning bush" moment, just like Moses had.

I remember whispering the words: "God? Please help me to forgive my dad." Those words felt nearly impossible at first, but in the blink of an eye, something remarkable happened. The weight on my heart began to lift from my chest. The bitterness that had once encompassed my entire existence, my entire life, started to lose its grip. Gradually, I experienced freedom—real, tangible, freedom. And I finally understood what Colossians 3:13 meant: "forbearing one another and, if one has a complaint against another, forgiving each other; as the Lord has forgiven you, so you also must forgive." Forgiveness became not only possible, but life-changing.

Brenton, this healing journey won't happen overnight. The weight has been lifted from you, but that doesn't mean you won't be reminded of it from time to time, and that's okay. It will require honesty, vulnerability, and patience with yourself and with others. It will demand bravery—the courage to face the pain you've carried and to trust God enough to surrender it fully into His hands. And remember, forgiving doesn't require you to excuse your father's decisions or pretend that the hurt never existed. Forgiveness just means handing your father—and your pain—over to God, trusting His justice, His grace, and His healing power. It means choosing to stop punishing yourself and others for the wounds only God can truly mend.

In time, you'll begin to see your father differently—not just as someone who hurt you, but as someone just as broken, flawed, hurt, and deeply in need of grace, just as you. This shift will not only heal your relationship with your past, but will also heal how you relate to others and yourself. The journey from anger and bitterness to forgiveness will also transform your relationship with God. You will see Him clearly as a Father who never leaves, never abandons, and always cares. His love is perfect, unchanging, and unconditional, unlike anything you've ever experienced. Trusting Him with your pain, anger, and bitterness allows Him to replace them with peace, compassion, and purpose.

As you move forward in this life, the freedom you gain from overcoming anger and bitterness will allow you to fully step into your calling. You'll no longer be afraid of failure, weighed down by resentment. Instead, you are now free to use your story of healing as a powerful testimony of God's grace. Your story—your healing—will become a source of hope for others battling the same pain.

Your pain matters, Brenton. Your heart matters. And your freedom matters deeply to God. Today, choose courageously. Choose to trust God with your anger and bitterness. Choose forgiveness. Choose peace. Choose freedom. Know that I am so proud of the man you are becoming. I promise, healing is ahead, and the path that you're on is leading to beauty, peace, and purpose beyond what you can currently imagine.

With all my love, compassion, and belief in your incredible strength,
Your Older Self

Anger was my closest companion for many years. It took root in the fertile soil of my heart, watered by resentment, disappointment, and bitterness stemming from my father's absence. I carried this anger quietly, secretly nurturing it until it became a storm I could no longer contain. It shaped how I viewed myself, others, and even God. Maybe you feel this too. Perhaps anger has been simmering beneath the surface of your life for years—unaddressed, unresolved, and often unacknowledged. Maybe you've carried bitterness as a shield, believing that holding onto your pain protected you from further hurt.

What I have learned over time is that bitterness and anger don't shield us; instead, they isolate us. It holds us captive, and it robs us of the peace and joy that God intended for each of us to enjoy. In this chapter, I want to share openly about my journey toward healing from anger and bitterness—how God met me in the darkest moments, and how He gently and powerfully taught me to release these painful emotions into his hands.

Anger is not inherently wrong. In fact, anger is often a natural response to injustice or pain. But unresolved anger is destructive. When left unchecked, anger grows into bitterness, poisoning our spirits and relationships. For me, anger was rooted in abandonment and neglect on the part of my father. It was his absence that created a wound I couldn't heal, and every reminder of his absence felt like pouring salt into an open wound. I grew angry, not just at him, but at God, myself, and the world. I carried that bitterness, believing that it was justified.

God began to teach me something transformative, and that I didn't see myself. The anger I felt toward my dad was deeply intertwined with grief. I was grieving the father I never had, the memories never made, and the validation I never received. Recognizing the root of my anger was the first significant step toward healing. What unresolved wounds or losses have I been feeding unknowingly? Are there any unspoken griefs beneath the surface that need acknowledgement?

There is a cost of holding onto that bitterness, did you know that? It's like drinking poison and expecting it to harm someone else. Bitterness damages us from within, tainting our perspectives, robbing our joy, and damaging our relationships with others and with God. Hebrews 12:15 speaks powerfully on this: "See to it that no one fail to obtain the grace of God; that no "root of bitterness" spring up and cause trouble, and by it the many become defiled." My bitterness toward my absent father impacted other areas of my life too: I struggled with trust, vulnerability, and intimacy. I unfairly projected my hurt onto other people who genuinely cared for me. Bitterness became the lens that distorted how I saw everything. God began to show me that holding onto bitterness didn't punish my father—it punished me. It imprisoned my heart in the past, preventing me from fully embracing the future God had for me.

Forgiveness was one of the hardest, yet liberating steps I ever took. Forgiveness didn't mean excusing my father's absence; it meant releasing my right to remain angry. It meant entrusting justice and healing to God, allowing His capable hands to achieve His end goal and not my own. God's word is an anchor in the most difficult of times, and my life was no different. Colossians 3:13 is one of those anchors: "forbearing one another and, if one has a complaint against another, forgiving each other; as the Lord has forgiven you, so you also must forgive." I remember the day I chose forgiveness vividly. Now, I didn't feel particularly forgiving right away—it was a conscious decision to trust God and release my anger— and it was that anger that I felt lift from my chest. Over time, my heart followed. Forgiveness is rarely a one-time event; rather, it's an ongoing journey, one choice at a time. The heart can contain only a finite amount, and choosing forgiveness began to free my heart from the bitterness it carried. It allowed me to heal and find peace.

An important thing to learn quickly is how to express this anger in healthy ways. Suppressed anger eventually—often explosively—causes further harm. I learned that anger is safest when expressed honestly to God and trusted individuals. The Psalms provided me a powerful blueprint on how to deal with raw, unfiltered emotions. God invites you to share your anger and pain honestly, without fear of rejection. He meets you with compassion, patience, and understanding. I learned to turn anger into powerful, honest prayer. And in those prayers, I was able to find profound healing in those sacred moments of vulnerability.

Compassion may seem impossible when anger and bitterness run deep, but it's essential for lasting healing. As God softened my heart, I began to see my father's brokenness clearly—not to excuse him, but to understand him. Compassion allowed me to let go fully, seeing my father as human, flawed, and hurting too. A man troubled by his own wounds, desperately trying to find relief from the pain by way of the vices he tried to use as a bandage. Once I began having that thought, I knew instantly that he deserved forgiveness too. Luke 6:36 calls us higher: "Be merciful, even as your Father is merciful." Compassion doesn't erase pain; it transforms it. Choosing compassion freed me to heal deeply, moving forward in love rather than bitterness. Please consider this: Could compassion toward those who hurt you change your healing journey?

Overcoming anger and bitterness isn't about mustering personal strength. You can't win this battle with sheer force, but only through surrender. It's about leaning into God's grace. He promises to heal broken hearts, to replace bitterness with peace, anger with grace, and pain with purpose. Psalm 147:3 beautifully promises: "He heals the brokenhearted, and binds up their wounds." I am inviting you to trust God's promise for healing. Allow Him to access your heart, no matter how deeply wounded it is.

Anger and bitterness no longer control the man that I am inside. They no longer represent me—God does. My journey taught me that freedom from bitterness is possible. The resentment I felt toward my father slowly faded away. Bitterness became compassion, anger became forgiveness, and resentment turned into a purpose. You are not alone in your journey. God sees you clearly, loves you deeply, and is committed to walking with you every step toward freedom.

Reflection Questions

1. What areas of your life have been the most affected by anger and bitterness?

2. Can you identify the wounds that fuel your anger? How can you begin addressing them?

3. What steps toward forgiveness and compassion can you take today?

Devotional Thought

"Let all bitterness and wrath and anger and clamor and slander be put away from you, with all malice, and be kind to one another, tenderhearted, forgiving one another, as God in Christ forgave you." — Ephesians 4:31-32

Books

- *Forgiving What You Can't Forget* by Lisa TerKeurst

- *The Bait of Satan* by John Bevere

- *Enemies of the Heart* by Andy Stanley

Music

- "Forgiveness" by Matthew West

- "Chain Breaker" by Zach Williams

- "Graves Into Gardens" by Elevation Worship

Chapter 10

PAINFUL TRUTHS AND THE OVERWHELMING POWER OF FORGIVENESS

D EAR Me,
     Fair warning. This letter will hurt because the time has come to talk about forgiveness. What's more, you've learned that forgiveness has different forms based on what you've experienced. You've learned the pain of betrayal, of imperfect people who've hurt you in some way due to their own unresolved hurt, the pain of unremorseful people who hurt twice over, the pain of self-realization that you've hurt others in these same ways, the pain of forgiving yourself for these wrongs, the pain of acceptance that reconciliation doesn't always come after forgiveness, and finally the pain of letting go of the need for justice or revenge. Each of these hurts in its own way, but it is possible to work through them with the right help.

Forgiveness is so much deeper than saying "I'm sorry" and walking away. Unfortunately, in our youth and inexperience, our grade school teachers had to set some expectations when people didn't get along, and I argue that it was too low. It isn't their fault; you can't expect a kid that age to understand the concept I am trying to explain because forgiveness goes much deeper than superficial wounds. So, in setting this expectation, they were only doing their best in the situation they found themselves in. As we got older, we grew. Our minds expanded, and we were able to build upon that expectation.

You've spent many nights questioning your value, your worthiness of love, and even your place in this world, all because of wounds inflicted by others. You've carried these hidden hurts, afraid that bringing them into the light would only make them more real, more painful. Yet, I want to gently assure you of something crucial: your pain matters deeply. It matters to God, it matters to me, and it's important enough to acknowledge openly, rather than hidden away in shame or fear

Here is the first painful truth, Bubba. You have been avoiding some hard truths in your life. You've hidden the pain you carry by lying to yourself and those you love. You ignore the people who have hurt you along the way by cutting them out of your life. And you've refused to acknowledge how you've hurt others by consistently trying to justify your actions and minimizing their effects. Of these things, you are guilty. But in the midst of all this, light shines upon you, and there is a way to make things right, freeing you from this prison of thought. You need to forgive yourself, forgive others, and then ask for and receive forgiveness from others for your actions if that option is present.

Sometimes, forgiveness feels impossible; I understand that. You have been betrayed by the one man who should have been the most important in your life. Forgiving him for what he did feels like a betrayal against yourself; a betrayal of justice. His actions have caused a wound so deep that no surgeon could ever mend it. And in your mind, you are battling the thought that he doesn't deserve your forgiveness. Here comes another painful truth, Brenton. You don't deserve forgiveness either; nobody does. Everyone who has walked on this planet, except one, is imperfect. Each is bound to make mistakes repeatedly until the day they die, and it is for this very reason that Jesus paid the price we couldn't pay so that we could receive forgiveness in God's eyes and join Him one day. My next question for you is simple. Are you going to forgive your dad and let go, or are you going to face God and have to account for why you refused to forgive when you received forgiveness? That seems unfair, and I fear the conversation with God, because you know He will hold you accountable for it.

Well, here is the next central point. One of the hardest lessons you will learn about forgiveness is that it's not about excusing what happened or pretending the hurt didn't matter. It is not about whether or not they deserve forgiveness. The craziest part is that it's about you! It's about releasing your fist that was ready to throw a punch. It's about releasing the pain in your heart and letting that poison drain out of you. It's about healing. You cannot experience the freedom of forgiveness when you have the ball and chain of anger and malice shackled to your ankle.

There's profound strength in vulnerability and honesty. Healing begins when we dare to speak the truth about our wounds, trusting God to step into the deepest, most painful places of our lives. Healing continues as we courageously choose forgiveness day after day, even when it's challenging or uncomfortable

Imperfection, coupled with the idea of whether someone deserves forgiveness, is the hardest thing you will learn to overcome. This idea isn't just a one-way thought, but applies reversely when you hurt others. One day, you will realize that nobody has all the answers and that they, too, have experienced life to such a degree that they are flawed too. You are holding onto anger and letting it build up, causing hatred to fester inside you, and it will lead you nowhere but rock bottom. It won't let go of your throat until you force it to by forgiveness. Holding someone to the impossible standard of perfection will only keep you trapped in disappointment. God commands that we forgive others just as He forgave us, but why? Forgiveness allows you to see their humanity, to see them as God does, and to free yourself from the need for them to be perfect.

Another harsh reality of this world is what happens when someone who has wronged you never apologizes or seeks forgiveness. In certain circumstances, the individuals who have hurt us move on and are no longer in our lives. Even if they wanted to, sometimes reconnecting for that purpose is impossible, and the reason doesn't matter. They could have moved to a different country, and the answer is still valid. Forgiveness is not dependent on an apology. God spoke about this in His Word. Pray. It's that simple. Pray to God and tell Him that you've chosen forgiveness. Ask Him to help you through the process, and also take into account the forgiveness you've chosen to give. God will sort things out later, and He can handle it. What has been done or said in secret will be known to the

Father. (Matthew 6) In this situation, please do not feel like your forgiveness and the healing inside that comes with it are falling on deaf ears or blind eyes. God can see everything.

I'm not done yet, Bubba. You've been hurt; that part is clear, but you have also hurt others. You've acted in anger, selfishness, and deceit; in doing so, you've hurt others sometimes without even realizing it. You've entered relationships with people with good intentions that you've ultimately burned to the ground because you were hurting. That's not an excuse; it's the reality. True forgiveness isn't just about releasing the grip you've had on others. It's about reaching deep to find a heavy dose of humility and seeking forgiveness for your own wrongdoings. Some of these relationships were romantic, so it's not about returning to a broken relationship or one that would now be inappropriate. It is simply about seeking forgiveness and moving on. If the person wishes to give that forgiveness, great! If not, then at least they know you tried to reconcile your wrongs, and hopefully, they come to these same terms. If they do, they will remember that awkward conversation you tried to have and attempted to reconcile. Forgiveness frees your heart, but sadly, reconciliation is not always the outcome, and it may seem unjust.

Justice is not what you think it is. You want justice. You want your "Aha!" or "Gotcha!" moment because you've been wronged. You're confused, though. You don't want justice; you're seeking vindication. Your "Aha!" moment is about showing others that you were hurt and that the other person is at fault. It has nothing to do with actual justice because actual justice weighs all the factors involved. That means that the aggravating factors increasing guilt will be considered, but mitigating factors that lessen guilt will also be considered.

The idea that forgiveness allows the other person to get away with hurting you is false. It is a lie. I dare to say that it is a lie of the evil one. The truth is that holding onto this need for retribution or revenge only sharpens the hurt. It's like acid on your skin, continuing to burn until you wash it off. Forgiveness does not allow an escape from justice. It is placing trust in God, knowing He sees the injustice and will handle it in His timing and in His way. You can let go of that burning desire for revenge by understanding that true justice rests in God's hands.

When you get to the point in life that you begin to have these thoughts, you will find that learning to forgive yourself is just as complicated, if not more so, than forgiving someone else. Shame and guilt are weapons of the enemy, trying to keep you suppressed long enough so that you begin to believe you don't deserve the forgiveness you've shown to others and that God has shown to you. Accepting grace means believing in His forgiveness and placing it in your life. It releases the burden of guilt and is about trusting God's love and mercy. Choose to live in this freedom, and don't hold yourself back.

Forgiveness is not weakness, by the way. I don't know why people think this. As we've already said, it's not giving in or pretending everything is okay. If anything, forgiveness is the hard path. Every day, we are faced with decisions, and each day, we can usually choose the easy way or the hard way. In this instance, forgiveness is the hard way. We are letting it go and trusting God instead. There is beauty in surrender. It is a conscious decision not to let the past control your future. Breaking free from bitterness and resentment is simultaneously choosing to heal everything else.

Forgiveness is a journey in both providing and receiving it. It never happens all at once, and it's not easy. Pray that God opens your memory because, as you progress through this journey, you will be surprised at the memories that come to mind. Memories that you have completely forgotten about. Sometimes, these memories also bring pain. In those moments, you will have to choose forgiveness again, but as you move forward, it will slowly become easier to accomplish because the weight is lifting from your shoulders.

The chains are gone, the weight is gone, and it is as if a beautiful sunrise on the horizon calls you into the freedom that awaits you. Sunrise is the hope and promise of a beautiful new day. This freedom to let go of the past is not because the pain never mattered; it is because you've made the conscious decision to learn from it, and use it as part of your story. You've chosen God's plans over your own. Take back your life, and trust God.

You need to start this process. Begin by forgiving your dad for what he did, or more specifically, what he didn't do. Seek out the forgiveness of others. The Lord knows you need to, even when it is difficult to admit it. Finally, forgive yourself too. Take the grace that the Lord freely gives you. You don't have to carry all this weight anymore. It's time to let it go and let God do what He does best. Remember, forgiveness isn't about the person who hurt you; it's about your healing, and you deserve to be free.

Your Older Self

Hey, Dad. I know you're reading this, and I'm using our relationship as my example for this chapter. It is important that you read this, but it is also important that I show my readers that I am a man of my word. But more importantly, you know what this chapter is about. I want you to know that I forgive you, Dad. I forgive you for all the birthdays, t-ball games, and choir concerts you missed. For those lonely days when I needed you, and you weren't there. For the times I needed your advice, but you weren't around to impart wisdom to me. The vast chasm of emptiness inside my heart that your absence created. Yeah, I forgive you for that, too. You may not have realized the depth to which your absence would impact me, and that isn't your fault. After we reunited, I struggled with it but never said anything. To this day, there are still some sticky points that I struggle with. But also, as you know, this book isn't about blame, but about what I found while you were gone. Despite all the pain, sorrow, and constant uphill battles I waged, I would do it again, knowing what I know now. Knowing that on the other side of this dark valley created by your absence, my Heavenly Father was preparing to bring me to the highest peak. He also took this time to introduce Himself to me, and I'm eternally grateful for that.

Today, I publicly repeat what has been the truth inside my heart for many years. I chose to release the hurt and bitterness I've carried against you. In private prayer to God, I've told Him that I've forgiven you, and in that silent prayer, He has heard me. I choose to let go of the weight of unmet expectations and the anger that has held me captive. I forgive you, not because it was easy or because the pain wasn't real, but because I wanted to be free. I wanted you to be free. I want to live a life where love and peace from God reign, and not the wounds of the past. If left to fester, the wounds will never fade. But through forgiveness, over time, those wounds will die. I hope one day, you'll understand the depth of this forgiveness and that it is rooted in the grace I've found in God. I know you also have faith in God, so I pray that He enhances that faith as deeply as you can feel it. As deeply as I have felt it. You've often said to me that you feel like I've missed my calling. You've felt that I should have entered the clergy for years and become a pastor. Maybe, maybe not … Nonetheless, this book has immense power. I've asked God to bless this work and to bring it to those who need it the most. As a wise priest once said, "When you walk with Jesus, you are never alone." Since I've dedicated this book to God, I can only imagine what He will do with it.

The journey of forgiveness is not just a single decision you make one day. It is an ongoing process of refinement that requires courage, vulnerability, and grace. At its core, forgiveness is a deeply personal act of releasing the power of pain and resentment over our lives. It is an invitation to step into healing, reclaiming the parts of us that bitterness and anger have stolen. The journey is not easy, and it often begins with facing painful truths, several of which I have personally experienced.

The pain of betrayal leaves a scar that can feel impossible to heal. It could be something similar to my story, where a parent abandons their responsibilities and violates their position in your life; it could be a friend breaking your trust or a spouse being unfaithful. No matter what it is, betrayal shakes the entire foundation of relationships. It doesn't just hurt — it changes us, making us question not only others' intentions but our own ability to trust. I remember the betrayal I felt when I realized that my father wasn't coming back, that he wouldn't be the protector and guide I desperately needed. It felt like the ground had fallen from underneath me. That was when the chasm formed in my heart.

That betrayal turned to anger, and over time, the anger hardened my heart into bitterness. I felt that by holding onto this bitterness, I was building a wall, never to allow another person to hurt me again. Writing this way makes my reaction sound so cliché, but it's what I felt at the time. In early 2010, I found myself at Naval Station Great Lakes, Recruit Training Command. Part of the process of molding yourself into a sailor is to memorize a lot of information. One of those items needed for memorization was the Recruit Maxim, which stated: "I will not lie, cheat, or steal, nor tolerate those among us who do." This has stuck with me not only because I memorized it, but because I connected it with my knowledge of the faith. I could see the maxim as the exact opposite of what Satan wants. The largest problem with bitterness is that it steals joy, hope, and connection. That is exactly what Satan does; he steals our joy by lying to us, he cheats us by tempting us to make decisions that hurt us and don't help us, or, probably his personal favorite, confuses us by taking scripture and misquoting it or misinterpreting it. Satan loves to sow bitterness because that is where he feels most comfortable. Forgiveness, in the face of the bitterness of betrayal, doesn't mean pretending it didn't happen. It's about recognizing that while the betrayal changed you, it doesn't have power over you. Forgiveness is reclaiming your ability to trust, not in people who have failed you, but in God, who never will.

This might come off as an excuse for bad behavior, and I promise it isn't. It is, however, the truth... A difficult concept to grasp is that people are flawed. We often hold those closest to us to the highest standards, expecting perfection where it is impossible. Parents, friends, mentors — they all make mistakes, sometimes at our expense. For a really long time, I saw my father through the lens of my hurt, expecting him to have been everything I needed and more. I wanted him to be perfect, to fix the pain he caused somehow retroactively.

As I grew, I slowly began to see him as a man with his own struggles and wounds that influenced his life choices. This didn't excuse his actions, but it helped me see how God sees him through the lens of grace. It was only in forgiveness that I could see him this way. It's funny how it happened like this. We are told to forgive not seven times but seventy times seven. God tells us to go on this journey of forgiveness, and now it makes sense why... God wants us to see each other as He sees us; like I said, only through forgiveness can I experience this next level of faith. Forgiveness in this context means letting go of the need for someone to have been perfect to be loved. It's about accepting that we're all in need of grace, and just as we hope others will forgive our imperfections, we're called to forgive theirs.

Since my dad wasn't around until I was almost a teenager, there was a long wait before he came back into my life. One of my deepest fears was the invasive thought that he would die before I was able to meet him. I wrestled with that one for a few years. When faced with the possibility that an apology would never come, what do you do with that, especially at such a young age? Some wounds cut us so deeply that we wait years —or even a lifetime—for an apology that may never come. For years, I waited for my father to say, "I'm sorry." I thought those words had magical properties that would be the key to my healing. But the words didn't come when I needed them to. I had to ask myself this very question. "Brenton, how long will you wait for the apology that may never come?" Some people will never understand how they hurt you, while others will never admit it. Your healing is not dependent on their seemingly empty words but entirely on a personal choice to let go and move forward. When I realized this, I said to myself, "Stop waiting for what he may not give. Set yourself free." Imagine my bittersweet happiness when I was able to meet him, reintroduce him into my life, and finally be able to reconcile. It is not lost on me that I was lucky to have that moment of reconciliation, so I deeply feel for those where this is impossible. Forgiveness is not about waiting for someone else to act — it's about taking control of your own peace. When we forgive others without an apology, we are placing trust in God to be the ultimate judge. We're choosing to release the chains that tie us to the pain and step into the freedom that God offers. It's not easy by any measure. What worthwhile thing is? But if you do this, it is liberating, because there is beauty in surrender.

I want to take a moment to call something out. Forgiveness and reconciliation are not the same thing. This is important to understand. Forgiveness is about releasing bitterness and choosing to heal, whereas reconciliation requires both parties to be willing to repair the relationship. Sometimes, that is impossible, and other times, it may not even be appropriate in that phase of life. For example, would it be appropriate to reconcile and continue in a friendship with an old flame while you're engaged to be married to someone else? No, of course not. I would argue that reconciliation can still happen for the sake of mutual healing, but you both must go your separate ways. Sometimes, what's done has been done, and while mutual forgiveness and healing have been achieved, the separation must remain. And therein lies the pain, the what-ifs, and the regret. These are powerful teachers, but unfortunately, you have to experience them to understand.

I've forgiven people who are no longer in my life, not because I wanted to bring them back into it, but because I didn't want their actions to hold power over me anymore. Forgiveness freed my heart, even when reconciliation wasn't an option at the time. This was especially true with my father. Forgiving him didn't magically restore our relationship to what I wish it could have been. But it did allow me to move forward without the weight of a what-if hanging around my neck.

Eventually, when you undergo intense self-reflection, you uncover your own guilt. This is especially true when you pray and ask God to uncover or reveal long-suppressed or forgotten memories. As much as others have hurt me, I've also been the cause of hurt. This was a painful truth to admit, both to myself and to you, my readers. It is important that I show you all of my transgressions, and not just what was good for this book. Maybe not in the most detail, but definitely so you know I'm not just standing on a soap box. Whether it was out of anger, fear, ignorance, deceit, or selfishness, I've said things and made decisions that left others feeling wounded. Recognizing this was one of the most humbling parts of my journey.

Sometimes, I lashed out at people who didn't deserve it. I would project my pain onto others, seemingly for no reason. There were relationships, romantic or otherwise, that I damaged or self-sabotaged because I didn't know how to process my own internal feelings. That hardened, bitter heart wouldn't allow me to feel romantic love for a long time. Owning these mistakes was not easy, but it was necessary. Seeking forgiveness from those you have wronged isn't just about healing those relationships — it's about freeing yourself from the guilt and shame of the past. It's a step toward becoming the person God created you to be, someone who walks in humility and grace. If forgiveness is not bestowed on you by the person you've wronged, then at least you tried to make it right.

When we are the ones who are wronged, what is our first response? We want retribution, right? We call it justice or even revenge. That is, to equalize our pain on both sides of the coin with the perpetrator. We follow the idea of Hammurabi's Code, "an eye for an eye." It is the idea that justice is defined as the punishment being equal to the crime. If you are honest with yourself and get over the initial emotional reaction to the crime, you will realize that this is not justice. Mahatma Gandhi is said to have said it best: "An eye for an eye makes the whole world blind." This goes back to what I said about how forgiveness can feel like we are letting them "get away with it." Holding onto that need only deepens the wound.

Many of you may have watched YouTube videos of courtrooms where a family member of someone horribly injured or killed forgives the person who committed the crime. Why does watching this pull the strings in our hearts? It is because we know deep down inside that forgiveness is the answer. It was written on our hearts long ago while God still formed us in our mother's womb. It stirs our hearts because it speaks to that deep-seated idea of forgiveness. I learned to let go of this need by trusting God to be the ultimate judge. Remember, He sees what is done privately, so He alone knows what is just. His justice is perfect, and ours is not.

I've said it once, and I'll say it again: Forgiveness does not mean the other person escapes accountability; it only means that you trust God to make the proper decision and to handle it in His way and His timing. Those YouTube videos are the perfect example… Upon the forgiveness of the family who was wronged, the judge doesn't bang the gavel and say, "Charges dismissed!" No, they still pass the sentence of the court's punishment while also weighing the idea and fact that the family has forgiven them of the crime. That is what a good judge does; they weigh all factors in their sentence.

As I've written about forgiving those who have wronged us and how difficult it is to do so, it can be even more demanding to do the next thing. One of the hardest truths I've faced is that I needed to forgive myself. We are our own worst judges. I held onto guilt and shame for so long, believing that my mistakes were too big to be covered by God's grace. Friends, this is a dangerous thing! Satan *loves* to confuse us in this way. Satan's goal is to keep us confused and in the dark. By not fully accepting the grace of God's forgiveness, we deny the same forgiveness He is offering us. Satan knows this, which is why he likes to keep throwing guilt and shame into our faces.

I am not a member of the clergy, and I've never been to seminary, but my layperson's knowledge of God's Word is that if we deny His grace, well, let's just say that it won't end up going well for us when we stand before God for judgment. We must fully humble ourselves before God, including every good and bad thing we committed, ask for forgiveness, and accept God's grace. If we don't, our sin remains. If, in some conceited way, we hold onto pride by holding ourselves responsible for something God has forgiven us for, we retain the punishment we feel we deserve.

Friends, forgiveness has never been about erasing the past — it's about reclaiming your future. If you've asked Jesus Christ into your heart and are baptized in the name of the Father, the Son, and the Holy Spirit, and are otherwise in full communion with the Church, you are a son or daughter of the Most High. The King of Kings, the Prince of Peace. That makes you an heir to His kingdom, so reclaim your place! You've been called by name. He has called your name, please, please answer Him. This is about choosing healing over bitterness, peace over anger, and freedom over the chains of resentment. Forgiveness isn't easy, but it's worth it. Each step forward will bring you closer to freedom, healing, and abundance. It is a journey that requires courage, but it leads to life in abundance. Trust Him with your journey.

Reflection Questions

1. Who do you need to forgive in your life, even if they've never apologized?

2. Are there people you've hurt who may be waiting for your apology?

3. What steps can you take to begin the process of forgiving yourself?

Devotional Thought

"Be kind and compassionate to one another, forgiving each other, just as in Christ God forgave you." — Ephesians 4:32

Reflect on how God's forgiveness has freed you, and how you can extend that same forgiveness to others.

Recommended Reading

- *"Total Forgiveness"* by R.T. Kendall

- *"The Gift of Forgiveness"* by Katherine Schwarzenegger Pratt

- *"Boundaries: When to Say Yes, How to Say No to Take Control of Your Life"* by Dr. Henry Cloud and Dr. John Townsend

Recommended Songs

- *"Forgiveness"* by Matthew West

- *"Come to the Altar"* by Elevation Worship

- *"Amazing Grace (My Chains Are Gone)"* by Chris Tomlin

Chapter 11

LEARNING TO EMBRACE
YOUR STORY

HEY Brenton,
It's me again. How many times have you wished for the opportunity for a do-over? I know your story isn't the one you would have chosen for yourself, or is it? I know how many nights you've spent awake, wishing you could rewrite chapters, erase painful pages, or simply start fresh. You look around and see people whose lives seem easier, whose stories seem less complicated, less messy, and you silently wonder why yours had to be different. Today, as I write these words to you, I want to gently remind you of something incredibly powerful: your story, with all its twists and turns, struggles, and triumphs, is deeply valuable—and entirely yours.

It is so tempting to try to hide bits and pieces of your story—especially the parts filled with shame, confusion, and pain. You've often believed that your experiences make you less lovable or somehow unworthy of good things. Yet, what you haven't realized yet is that those very experiences, those pages that you'd rather rip out and burn, are the ones that God will one day use in the most profound ways. Your greatest struggles hold within them your greatest opportunities for compassion, healing, and purpose.

Learning to embrace your story doesn't mean celebrating the hurt or pretending it wasn't difficult. It means courageously accepting where you've been, in the heat of those battles and despite their messiness, recognizing who you're becoming, having triumphed over those experiences.

I want you to boldly believe that your future is not limited by your past. Embracing your story means that you are allowing yourself to authentically be seen—not just in those moments of strength and success—but also in the moments of vulnerability, pain, and healing.

I remember how you used to think that if anyone saw the real story of our life—the messy parts, the wounds, and especially the absence of our dad—they might turn us away as nothing more than an orphan on the street. Mom was still around, of course, but without the literal other half of me present in my life, I still felt like an orphan. I remember this feeling most of all. It was dark, and it led my mind to places that I don't want to put in writing. It made me feel like I was good for nothing more than cannon fodder. When I thought about Tiffany and Joshy and how their lives came together with purpose, it made me want to copy them. I mean, their choices were working for them, so why wouldn't they work for me? It made me want to blend in rather than stand out. But copying them would've been taking the easy road.

Eventually, I grew out of that and wanted to be everything they weren't. I wanted to blaze my own trail so I had something of my own to be proud of. Dare I say, I wanted something to shove in my dad's face and say: "Look what I did without your help!" I felt I had to prove myself somehow. That thought came from the version of me prior to forgiving him, so don't get confused. It was precisely those difficult experiences and thoughts that ultimately connected me deeply to others. When I found the courage to be honest and vulnerable, my story became a bridge rather than a barrier.

I remember hearing a sermon about wisdom. It was impactful, and it led to many conversations with God. Ultimately, in those conversations, I asked God to bestow wisdom on me. I remember that prayer, and I also remember not feeling wise immediately after. As they say, you have to be careful what you pray and ask for, because He might give it to you, just not in the way you expected. It's okay to laugh at that, I know I did when I looked back and remembered it. When I thought back on that prayer, it hit me—my wounds became the wisdom that I sought. The broken places within you are not signs of weakness or failure; they are signs of resilience, of survival, and of God's faithful presence even in the darkest chapters. Each scar has allowed me to tell this story to an audience who is willing to listen, and God willing, it can be millions! A physical reminder for each reader that healing, strength, and grace from God are evidence that He carried you through it the entire time.

Brenton, embrace this story that God has entrusted to you. He entrusted it to you for a reason; He had plans for you. Hiding or denying the past won't bring the peace and freedom you seek. True freedom will come when you bravely accept where you've been, when you choose compassion for yourself in your journey, and when you offer your experiences up to God, trusting Him to redeem every part of the story.

I know that you are a people person. You love to hear the stories of others because you know the truth about each person's story—they are uniquely powerful. Our stories hold within us the incredible power to inspire hope in others. Just as someone else's journey once gave you the courage, your honesty will one day become a beacon of hope for someone else who desperately needs to hear that they are not alone.

Psalm 139:14 reminds us: "I praise thee, for thou art fearful and wonderful. Wonderful are thy works! Thou knowest me right well." God knows your story intimately, every chapter, every line, every word—and He calls it wonderful, not because it was always easy, but because through every part of it, you were never alone. He has seen your heartache, your doubts, your triumphs, and your courage. He deeply values every detail of who you are and where you've been.

The journey of embracing your story involves releasing shame, guilt, and regret. It means stepping forward in courage, knowing that your past does not write the story of your future. It means believing that you are profoundly loved, not in spite of your experiences, but precisely because they've shaped you into someone compassionate, wise, and incredibly resilient. Embracing your story also means understanding that your identity isn't rooted in what you've experienced—it's rooted in who God declares you to be: chosen, redeemed, and beloved. When you see yourself through this lens, you'll find freedom you've never experienced before—a freedom to share your story openly, authentically, and without fear.

I can't promise that embracing your story will always be easy. There will be moments when shame resurfaces, when old wounds remind you of past hurts, or when fear whispers that your story is too broken to matter. During these moments, lean deeply into God's promise in Romans 8:28: "We know that in everything God works for good with those who love Him, who are called according to His purpose." Your life, every chapter, is part of something greater in store, something that you cannot currently see.

As you begin to accept your story fully, you'll discover opportunities to help others embrace their own. Your honesty will give permission to others to be honest. Your courage will inspire courage. Your healing will encourage healing. Your willingness to share your story will set others free to embrace their own. Younger me, your life is a masterpiece, still being painted by a loving God. The messy parts aren't flaws—they're beautiful brushstrokes contributing depth, strength, and authenticity to your portrait. Trust the Artist. Trust that even the painful strokes are part of something incredible that He is creating.

As you continue forward, choose authenticity over perfection, vulnerability over hiding, and grace over shame. Embrace this journey fully, with all the complexity, beauty, and redemption that it has to offer. Your story matters deeply—not just to you, but to countless others who will find hope, courage, and healing because you chose to share it.

I'm deeply proud of you—for who you are, for where you've come from, and for the extraordinary story you're courageously embracing each day. You are stronger than you realize, wiser than you give yourself credit for, and so deeply loved. Keep trusting God. Keep embracing your story. Keep believing that there is a powerful purpose awaiting you.

With endless love, pride, and hope,
Your Older Self

For a long time, my story felt like something I needed to hide. It embarrassed me. It was something that I needed to bury beneath carefully constructed smiles and neatly packaged answers. Growing up without a father created complexities and wounds I wasn't ready to face openly. I believed that embracing my story meant giving power to the pain. It seemed easier, safer even, to hide behind silence and pretend certain chapters didn't exist. But I learned over time—and through much struggle—that my story is not something to be ashamed of. It's not something I had any control over. It's not something to erase or rewrite. It's something that should be acknowledged fully, embraced courageously, and surrendered completely into God's hands. Your journey, with all its highs and lows, forms the foundation of your strength, compassion, and wisdom.

In this chapter, I wanted to share how I learned to stop hiding from my past and how I started embracing my story in its entirety. Together, we'll explore what it means to honor each chapter God has written for us, and how embracing our stories helps others embrace theirs.

I believed that vulnerability equaled weakness. I feared that if people truly knew the depth of my struggles, my own family included, that the feelings of abandonment, the pain of rejection, the uncertainty about my self-worth, they would reject me too. I hid my hurt behind walls of strength and pretended to be unaffected by the absence of my dad. Yet, deep down, I longed to be known, understood, and accepted just as I was. I didn't realize that vulnerability was the key to the meaningful conversations and connections I so desperately wanted. It took many lonely, painful years for me to realize that authenticity, even in the broken parts of my story, was powerful.

One day, in a moment of deep honesty, I shared my full story with a friend. I spoke openly about my father's absence. I spoke about my doubts, my fears, and my unending questions. I shared that I questioned God's presence during those painful seasons. To my surprise, instead of judgment, I received understanding, empathy, and genuine compassion. It was then that I realized an important truth: vulnerability opens the door for healing—not just for us, but for those who hear our stories. When we share openly, we allow others to realize they're not alone. As scripture reminds us: "My grace is sufficient for you, for my power is made perfect in weakness." (2 Corinthians 12:9) God works most profoundly in our most vulnerable moments, turning our weakness into beautiful testimonies of grace. So, what are some fears or beliefs that are holding you back from being vulnerable about your story?

Shame often convinces us that our stories are unworthy of sharing—that they're too messy, complex, flawed, or too broken. One of the devil's favorite tools is to use shame against us in any situation that he can. To keep us oppressed as much as he can, so that the comforting Word of God cannot get out. For years, it was this exact shame that kept me silent. That shame told me that my father's absence somehow represented me, that it made me somehow less lovable and less valuable. It took courage and intentional work to recognize those lies and replace them with God's truth.

Romans 8:1 says, "There is now no condemnation for those who are in Christ Jesus." It took time, prayer, and intentional surrender to believe this fully. But as I embraced God's unconditional love, the weight of shame began to lift. My story shifted from something shameful to something redeemed by God's grace. Learning to embrace your story requires embracing grace, not just from God—though that is important—but also by extending grace to yourself. It means believing your experiences don't disqualify you from love; they qualify you uniquely to speak hope into the lives of others who share similar struggles. How can you extend grace to yourself regarding the parts of your story you've carried with shame?

It took quite a while to understand that the experiences I once viewed as liabilities and baggage were actually incredible assets. My difficult experiences, particularly my struggle with fatherlessness, became opportunities to connect deeply with others who suffered from similar wounds. The vulnerability I feared most became my greatest strength. I remember one night when I was in college, I attended a regular Wednesday night meeting of Intervarsity Christian Fellowship. We spoke about a topic that ignited a storm within me, and I ended up staying up until 2 am the next morning, sharing my story with another student. He expressed gratitude that I was vulnerable enough to share it with him.

I spoke openly about the pain, confusion, and healing that I'd experienced and that I was still undergoing. Afterward, one by one, I began sharing that same story with more of my friends. They too found shared powerful stories of their own to share, once they knew the space they were in was a safe one. Several of them came to me privately afterward, expressing gratitude for my honesty and the opportunity to share theirs. It was in those moments with these friends that I discovered the true power of storytelling—especially stories that are filled with vulnerability and truth.

Your story has this same incredible power. It holds the ability to reach places in the hearts of people that otherwise would be dark. Polished perfection, or rather the illusion of it, would never have been able to reach these places. It never would have discovered these stories and potentially led some of those friends to healing they never knew was possible. That confidence in knowing that there is light shining upon us is unexplainable. Have you ever considered how your experiences could bring hope or encouragement to someone else?

Believing that your painful experiences serve a higher purpose is essential in embracing your story. Some shrug this off in frustrated depression, pushing God away from His rightful place in our lives. Please don't be one of them. Let God do what He does best, because nothing you've endured is wasted in God's hands. Each challenge that you've met has hurt deeply, but in that struggle, you will find the potential for powerful redemption and purpose.

The Bible promises us in Romans 8:28: "We know that in everything God works for good with those who love Him, who are called according to His purpose." While it's difficult to trust Him in these moments of pain, I've personally experienced it. I've witnessed this struggle in others. I have experienced the pain, so I can see it in the eyes of others. Probably the most amazing thing about this journey is the ability to witness God transform my hurt into opportunities for ministry, connection, and a deepening of faith.

Brenton, your story—with all its complexities—is part of something beautiful that God is crafting. Your experiences uniquely qualify you to minister to others, offering comfort, empathy, and hope from a place of genuine understanding. Trusting God means believing that every chapter matters—even the difficult ones. How have you seen or imagined God redeeming your painful experiences for good?

Most of the time, when I struggled to express all that I've written here, I found it extremely difficult to wrap my head around how to articulate this specific chapter. How do I get you to understand the importance of embracing our story so that you, one day, become the man writing this book? I always thought that it was abstract, but it isn't; it involved incremental steps of courage and authenticity:

- **Share with Safe People** — Find trusted individuals who offer empathy and understanding. Sharing your story builds courage to share more openly over time.

- **Journal Honestly** — Writing privately about your experiences provides clarity and releases emotional weight. Honesty on paper often precedes honesty in person. Who knows? Maybe your journal will become a book one day.

- **Practice Self-Compassion** — You need to treat yourself with kindness, recognizing that your story has value despite its difficulties. Self-compassion fuels courage. Additionally, it is no secret that we tend to speak to ourselves in the harshest ways. In ways that we would *never* speak to others, and that needs to stop. Today.

- **Surrender to God** — Regularly surrender your experiences to God, asking Him to heal, redeem, and use them.

- **Take Small Risks** — Gradually sharing small portions of your story publicly helps build confidence, leading to deeper authenticity.

Today, I no longer hide my past, my struggles, my pain, my mistakes, or the hurt that I've caused others. Instead, I embrace them openly, trusting that God uses each experience to shape me and bless others. My journey from hiding to authenticity wasn't easy, but it was worth every uncomfortable conversation. Your story, too, is sacred. It holds meaning, purpose, and power beyond your imagination. God has uniquely shaped you, through your experiences, to bring encouragement and hope to others who need exactly what you have to offer.

Embrace your journey, not with reluctance or shame, but with courage, grace, and faith. Your past doesn't determine your worth as a human being —it magnifies God's faithfulness in your life. Stand confidently in your truth, knowing that God sees your story as beautiful, valuable, and full of divine potential. May you always remember this: your story matters deeply, exactly as it is, and embracing it will unlock possibilities you never dreamed possible.

Reflection & Application

Reflection Questions

1. What parts of your story have you been hesitant to share or embrace?

2. How might your vulnerability bring hope to others?

3. What step will you take this week to embrace your story more fully?

Devotional Thought

"I praise thee, for thou art fearful and wonderful. Wonderful are thy works! Thou knowest me right well." – Psalm 139:14 (RSV-CE)

Recommended Resources

Books

- *Daring Greatly* by Brené Brown

- *Emotionally Healthy Spirituality* by Peter Scazzero

- *The Gift of Being Yourself* by David G. Benner

Music

- "Beautiful Things" by Gungor

- "Scars" by I AM THEY

- "Known" by Tauren Wells

Chapter 12

HEALING FATHER WOUNDS IN PERSONAL AND ROMANTIC RELATIONSHIPS

D EAR Younger Me,
I've thought deeply about the words I'm sharing with you today. I understand your feelings, and I know how deeply personal and painful they can feel. As I reflect on our journey, I understand exactly how the absence of our father has impacted you. There are so many layers of life that were violated—especially in relationships—both personal and romantic in nature. Confusion and frustration ran rampant throughout your life as you struggled to relate to others. You struggled to trust, you wondered whether you were worthy of love, and you desperately tried to fill voids that you didn't fully understand.

I can see clearly now the impactful influence that Dad's absence left on us—not just in our relationship with him, but in how we connect to everyone else in our lives. We carried a wound that colored each interaction we had with another human being, and we often didn't even realize it. Trust is a difficult thing to give for someone like us—someone who was betrayed at such a young age. As such, it affected how we decided to trust others, how deeply we allowed ourselves to be known, and how readily we accepted love or pushed it away out of fear.

I know those questions that I've mentioned in these writings already make yet another appearance here… "Am I able to be loved?" "Am I good enough?" "Everyone will leave me eventually, won't they?" These questions echoed loudly within your mind, making trust difficult, intimacy uncomfortable, and vulnerability terrifying. Relationships that should have brought joy and happiness only brought confusion and a general feeling of being unsafe. I wish I could have been there earlier to reassure you of this truth: these struggles are not reflections of your worth. Your worth is declared by God Himself, so don't worry about that part. The struggles are just natural responses to those deep wounds left by someone who was supposed to love, protect, and nurture you but chose instead to be absent. Believe it or not, you'll thank him one day for making that choice given the alternative, but that's a story for later.

It is important to know that Dad's absence does not limit your ability to love or be loved. Sure, his absence left wounds—but those wounds do not have the final say in your story. Remember, God used those wounds to get you to where I am today. Don't hate them, they serve a greater purpose. Healing is not only possible, but it's already underway! This entire time, God has been gently and patiently at work in your heart. He has been bringing clarity and compassion, even in those moments of deepest confusion and loneliness.

Now, you may wonder, as I once did, why healing seems slow and treacherous. Healing a wound as deep as this one is not an overnight process—it's a journey that requires courage, honesty, and trust. It's interesting to know that those are the exact things you've struggled with this entire time. They are the antidote to the poison of a father wound. As you well know, this process involves the unpacking of painful experiences, unlearning false beliefs about yourself, and allowing God access to your heart so that He can redefine your worth and value to His decree —especially in relationships. This journey wasn't easy, but it makes me wonder why God entrusted me with it. I'm not going to lie to you, it makes me feel powerful knowing that the God who can see everything entrusted this challenge to me. Maybe He wanted me to write this book, and maybe He has an incredible plan with it. One thing I know for sure is this: this journey is profoundly beautiful, transformative, and freeing. Getting these words onto paper has been helpful in my journey with God.

I think that the hardest lesson for me was realizing that I hurt other people along the way as a result of the wounds my father's absence left within me. I've broken friendships and romantic relationships, burning the bridges down as I left. I deeply regret those actions, and I hope that any of the ex-friends or ex-girlfriends reading this are willing to accept my apology for that. I sincerely didn't mean to, despite that's what it looked like. My insecurity sometimes manifested as jealousy or controlling behaviors. I struggled to trust others because, deep down, I expected everyone to eventually leave me, just like my dad did. It was a protection and coping mechanism I built for myself. If I expected the worst to happen, it didn't surprise me when it did. I now question myself, saying: "How could you live in this thought and expect success?!" For that, I have no answer, no excuse. I built those walls around my heart, unintentionally pushing away the very love and respect I longed so deeply for. What an oxymoron of a life!

I can recall clearly specific moments with specific people where my father wounds were evident. For example, when a friend showed genuine concern, only for me to feel skeptical and suspicious of their motives. I assumed they had hidden intentions or would soon abandon me. Instead of leaning into those friendships, I distanced myself, believing isolation was safer than potential rejection. The fear of abandonment morphed into patterns of emotional withdrawal, unintentionally hurting those who truly cared.

In romantic relationships, this pattern intensified. When someone would express genuine love and care for me, fear often took over. It wasn't long after the "I love you's" started being said that I began the fear cycle. Instead of embracing their affection, I subconsciously questioned their sincerity, convinced that sooner or later, they would see something in me that would make them want to leave. I can remember specific instances where I would create conflict or distance myself emotionally, almost as if I was testing their affection—pushing them away before they had a chance to abandon me. It is those actions that hurt me the most these days, knowing that I also hurt them.

When I deployed to the Middle East as part of my service in the US Navy, this fear became real. I was dating someone special to me at the time, and I was making progress through my fear cycle. This time, it was significantly more difficult due to the distance and nature of my absence. I received notification from a man who had been with her while I was away, and it wasn't until someone told him about me that he started to look into it. He confessed what happened and said that he didn't know. I believed him, but it ruined that relationship. It was probably the most significant setback I had experienced up until then. I'm happy to report that healing still happened. Several years later, she reached out to me with an apology. She recognized the pain she caused me and sought out reconciliation. I'm preaching the exact same thing in this book, so of course, I forgave her, and we went our separate ways.

Sometimes, I became overly critical, quick to find faults or reasons to justify pulling away. Other times, I became overly dependent on their affection, desperately seeking reassurance, yet never fully believing the love offered was genuine. That clinginess was often the reason they ended things. They wanted a relationship with a man, not a boy who had an absent father and who was left to mop up the emotional mess that it caused, and I don't blame them. All of these behaviors stemmed from the same deep-seated emotional scars. My father's absence wired my brain to believe that the people who claimed to love me would eventually leave, and I acted accordingly, often without realizing it.

I share this not to condemn you, but to offer compassion and reassurance. If you've seen yourself act in ways you regret, know that you're not alone, and you're certainly not beyond redemption. God's grace is sufficient, even in these messy, complicated places. Acknowledging our wounds and mistakes isn't about feeling shame; it's about inviting healing, freedom, and deeper, more authentic relationships into our lives. There is a powerful freedom to be had that comes when you choose to face your wounds with open honesty. As you do, you will begin to understand that the fears you've carried about abandonment and rejection don't have to hold you captive anymore. You will discover the incredible strength and joy found in vulnerability and authenticity. You will learn that love is possible—not just love given, but love received freely, without suspicion, hesitation, or fear.

In my journey toward healing, one truth became clearer than any other: the deepest healing comes from understanding and accepting God's perfect, unwavering love. Holy Scripture reminds us powerfully in Jeremiah 31:3: "I have loved you with an everlasting love; therefore I have continued my faithfulness to you." God's love is not dependent on performance, perfection, or even the ability to trust Him. His love remains steadfast through every moment, every mistake, and every fear. When you allow God's love to fill the void your father left within you, you'll find yourself less dependent on the approval or affirmation of others. You'll begin to enter relationships from a place of security rather than fear, and from love rather than neediness. This shift will transform everything you feel about relationships.

I can't wait for you to experience what I experience today. You will understand soon that one of the most beautiful outcomes of your healing journey will be the depth and richness it brings to your relationships— friendships, family connections, and romantic relationships alike. Healing these father wounds will allow you to break the patterns of pain. By breaking those patterns, you will develop new patterns of love and grace. There will be challenges, of course. Moments will come when old fears resurface, and when wounds you thought were healed remind you they're still tender. But in those moments, instead of feeling the shame and frustration so familiar to you, you will lean deeply into God's grace. Healing isn't linear, and setbacks don't spell disaster. With each step forward, no matter how small, each will bring you closer to the wholehearted life God desires for you.

As you continue to heal, you'll also begin to see your story as an incredible tool for encouraging and supporting others. Your experiences uniquely qualify you to offer compassion and hope to those walking similar paths. Your courage to face and heal these wounds will inspire others to do the same and find that courage within themselves. It is important that at each sunrise, you remind yourself that you are worthy of love. You are worthy of love not because someone chose to stay, and not because you've somehow earned approval—but because you are God's beloved child. God woke you up for another day for a reason. Your worth is already established by Him. Your worth does not fluctuate with human acceptance or rejection. God declares you fully known, fully loved, and fully accepted. This truth will anchor you as you navigate future relationships.

Remember that healthy relationships begin with a healthy understanding of yourself. This is why people take time between relationships to reintroduce themselves to their inner person. As you allow healing to transform your heart, your relationships will reflect that transformation. Love will become less about fear and more about joy, less about control of the unknown and more about freedom, and less about striving for survival and more about peace.

Your story isn't over. God has written so many beautiful chapters full of love, connection, healing, and redemption. Embrace this healing journey wholeheartedly, knowing that you are not alone, because remember that when you walk with Jesus, you are never alone. I promise that freedom, peace, and joy await you—along with relationships more meaningful, authentic, and fulfilling than you've ever imagined.

With endless love, compassion, and belief in the journey ahead,
Your Older Self

Father wounds affect more than just your relationship with your absent father—they seep into every relationship you'll ever have. From friendships to romantic relationships, the hurt of abandonment, rejection, or emotional distance can manifest in patterns you may not initially recognize. In my journey, I learned firsthand how deep these wounds run, but also how powerful healing can be when you begin addressing these wounds out in the open.

In this chapter, I want to share some knowledge in the hope that you can clearly see the ways father wounds might be influencing your personal and romantic relationships, while also offering hope and practical guidance on how to heal and build stronger, healthier connections.

Recognizing the common patterns that father wounds take is a crucial first step. Since father wounds tend to have a pattern, it can be easier to recognize their involvement in conflicts or personal issues once you are able to recognize them at a glance:

1. **Difficulty Trusting Others** — A father is charged by God with the responsibility to protect and care for his family. This truth is ingrained in us at the deepest, most unexplainable levels, which is why there is such a clear cause and effect relationship when it doesn't happen as it is supposed to. It is the fact that we "just know" that's how it's supposed to be! We begin to lose trust in almost everything. You may constantly question the motives of another, assuming eventual hurt, abandonment, or pain. This comes directly from the fact that your father, someone who was supposed to be trustworthy, wasn't there to lead you and fulfill his God-given role in your life.

2. **Fear of Abandonment** — One of the most common fears stemming from father wounds, and the most common in my personal experience, is that of a fear of abandonment. For many relationships in my youth, I subconsciously felt like each one had an expiration date. I felt that there would come a time when I would have to "move on," despite not really having a reason to. You may find yourself withdrawing or pushing people away prematurely, attempting to control

when the abandonment happens rather than the alternative of being emotionally hurt when it happens unexpectedly. Even in the most mundane things, I rarely am able to go enjoy a movie at the theater by myself, because I desire the connection of another so deeply. I cannot stand being alone.

3. **Overdependence or Emotional Isolation** — Probably the worst feeling of all is how my emotions swung back and forth like a pendulum. It either caused me to seek excessive validation, typically because I lacked self-esteem and self-confidence, or being so emotionally dependent on others that it damaged the relationship, furthering the hurt I experienced. This caused me to retreat into isolation and led me to convince myself that I don't need anyone in my life.

4. **Challenges with Emotional Intimacy** — Fathers are desperately needed in the family structure because they model certain characteristics in important ways, especially vulnerability, emotional intimacy, and processing adversity. Without a healthy father relationship to model vulnerability, emotional intimacy can be uncomfortable or even threatening. You may hide your true feelings or put up walls that limit authentic connection with someone. It is important to note that mothers and fathers are both equally and vitally important. While this book is specifically about a father's absence, due to my personal story, each parent models important attributes to their children. Often, the model has the same attributes and characteristics, but in complementary ways, so **never** think that one parent is more important than the other.

I recognized these patterns in my life after facing several failed relationships—both friendships and romantic connections. I often blamed the other person or simply believed I wasn't meant to have meaningful relationships. It took significant reflection to realize that my unresolved father wounds were silently sabotaging my connections with others. In romantic situations, I remember moments when someone expressed genuine affection to me, and I pushed it away. I was suspicious of how it felt. My heart racing, my breathing shallow, and my nervousness about sharing something as simple as a kiss was something completely foreign to me.

I often created emotional distance to protect myself from emotional pain, and I manufactured conflict out of minuscule issues to test whether the other person was loyal. There are several people I have in mind specifically, so if you're reading this, please understand that I never meant it as intentional cruelty. That's how I see it now, and the thought of causing that cruelty in your life hurts me to this day. I beat myself up about it, constantly. So, I ask that you take this book as both my explanation and my apology. It's important for me that you know there were things hidden under the surface that I just wasn't ready to let go of yet.

These behaviors were nothing more than defense mechanisms born out of deep-seated fear, sadness, and darkness in my life. When I began to address them honestly and out in the open, I found compassion. Compassion for myself and empathy for others whom I had intentionally hurt. Recognizing these patterns helped make it possible for me to take those initial meaningful steps toward healing.

The fact that romantic relationships amplify the effects of father wounds can be an interesting concept to understand. This is due to the fact that these relationships require deep trust and vulnerability. I saw my father wounds impact my romantic relationships in three ways:

1. **Fear-Based Decision Making** — Driven by uncontrolled fear and anxiety, my decision-making process was often hijacked. The fear of rejection, the fear of abandonment, and the fear of being unloved all played a role. As I mentioned earlier, I would leave relationships prematurely, or stay in unhealthy ones out of desperation, rather than confidence or clarity.

2. **Struggling with Commitment** — Even though I deeply desired an intimate connection with people, the anxieties made it difficult to fully commit. I wasn't emotionally available to make these connections sincerely.

3. **Unhealthy Expectations** — If you can read between the lines of what I've written thus far, you can see that I was left expecting nothing less than perfection because of my father wounds. A single mistake, or a comment made in a tone that I didn't find friendly, would immediately set off the fuse I have described. It placed unfair pressure on my relationships, ultimately leading to dissatisfaction and frustration. It burned bridges with people I would prefer to maintain a cordial relationship with, even to this day, because I enjoyed them as a person, just not romantically.

When I faced these realities, I realized that I had to be the change—not just my behavior, but my beliefs about myself, others, and relationships overall. Healing isn't quick or simple, but it's deeply rewarding. It often involves reopening wounds that you've buried in order to allow for proper processing. I needed a process to get me where I wanted to be, so this is what I did:

1. **Facing Your Story Honestly** — Healing begins with honesty. You need to recognize and admit your wounded and recognize how the wounds impact your relationships. This creates space for genuine change. Be patient with yourself in this process; honesty requires courage and vulnerability.

2. **Practicing Vulnerability** — Though vulnerability feels risky, it is essential for intimacy. Slowly sharing your feelings, fears, and hopes with trustworthy people builds emotional intimacy and helps to overcome isolation.

3. **Choosing to Forgive** — Forgiving my absent father didn't erase my hurt, but it did release the bitterness that harms my heart, and in turn, my relationships. Forgiveness frees you to heal and move forward in peace. Remember, it doesn't condone the behavior, but it releases the situation to God for His judgment because He can see what was done and spoken in secret.

4. **Counseling and Professional Support** — Professional counseling and therapy were transformative for me. Therapists trained in family dynamics and trauma can offer you valuable guidance. They can help you untangle complex emotions, identify harmful patterns, and build healthier relationships. Don't let financial difficulties get in the way either. There are usually local resources that can help you afford treatment.

5. **Leaning into God's Love** — Ultimately, healing came from accepting God's unconditional love as my foundation. Understanding my worth in God's eyes, not based on human validation, allowed healthier, more secure relationships. Jeremiah 29:11 says: "For I know the plans I have for you, says the Lord, plans for welfare and not for evil, to give you a future and a hope." God desires healing, joy, and fulfilling relationships for you.

Though father wounds impact your relationships profoundly, they do not have the final say. Your past will never inhibit your ability to experience love, trust, and genuine intimacy unless you allow it to. Healing, transformation, and healthy relationships are entirely possible. God's heart for you is healing, not brokenness; redemption, not rejection. Embrace this journey with courage, openness, and hope, believing fully that your relationships can flourish beyond expectation.

You are not alone. Your healing journey matters deeply, not only for you but for those you love and those who love you. As you heal, your relationships will become richer, deeper, and more meaningful. Your courage to heal your father wounds will inspire healing in others for the wounds they experience. It creates a ripple effect across humanity; a ripple effect of restored relationships, powerful connections, and transformative love.

Your journey toward God and your journey toward healing in your relationships are sacred, valuable, and entirely possible. God is still writing your story, and He isn't done with you yet. Each morning, if you wake to witness another sunrise, it is God telling you that a new day has come to accomplish everything He has in store for you. Take advantage of these opportunities, and see them in a positive light.

God's grace is sufficient, and His love is powerful enough to heal every wound and restore every broken piece of your heart. Keep believing in Him, keep trusting in Him, and keep healing in Him, no matter the situation. You may feel lost in a maze with no way out, but from His perspective, He can see the path you need to take. Your story is beautiful despite its content, and your future relationships will reflect the powerful healing that is bound to happen within you if you just say yes to Him.

Reflection & Application

Reflection Questions

1. Which relational patterns influenced by father wounds resonate most strongly with you?

2. How has fear of abandonment affected your relationships?

3. What's one practical step you can take today toward relational healing?

Devotional Thought

"The Lord is near to the brokenhearted, and saves the crushed in spirit." – Psalm 34:18 (RSV-2CE)

Recommended Songs for Healing

- "Reckless Love" by Cory Asbury

- "Known" by Tauren Wells

- "Run to the Father" by Cody Carnes

Chapter 13

NAVIGATING PARENTHOOD
WITHOUT A MODEL

H EY Brenton!
The next chapter in your life begins soon, because I know what is on the horizon. She just told you, and you were so in shock; you didn't know what to say. That's okay, the joy will come soon enough. But I also know that you are standing at a crossroads. On one hand, the thought of becoming a father feels so exciting. There is so much you're looking forward to. On the other hand, you're terrified that you'll become your father, making mistakes of your own and repeating the cycle you've felt your whole life. You know that is the last thing you could do to your baby girl. But I understand that you're scared.

Beneath the anticipation and dreams of raising a family of your own lies an underlying uncertainty. You have wondered quietly if it's even possible for you to be a good father when you didn't have the paternal example in your childhood to guide you. You asked yourself: "How can I be good at something that I never experienced at that age?" You were so worried about carrying on those same painful patterns. You felt inadequate, and at first, you couldn't stomach the idea that you could potentially cause the same pain you felt so deeply and for so long.

I understand these fears—because I was right there with you this whole time.

When I first became a father, I was overwhelmed with joy—but also with anxiety. Anxiety about my abilities as a father, as well as my anxieties about caring for Tiffany post-partum and assisting her as much as possible, contributed to the mental health issues in those first few months. My heart was full of love, but quiet fears echoed in my mind: "What if I screw this up?" "What if I make the same mistakes Dad did?" I was concerned that my lack of experience with a father figure would render me ineligible to be a good father. It left me feeling like I'd be stumbling around in the dark, unsure how to nurture, love, and guide another human being.

Thankfully, when Tiffany and I got together, I inherited two bonus kids. Elizabeth and Michael have been nothing but a joy and blessing, and even though I'm their stepfather, they've never cared about that fact. We've just been family, and that was an amazing feeling. With those two in my life, I got some practice in fatherhood. It was by no means perfect or easy by any definition, and I made plenty of mistakes that I had to apologize for, but the process was educational on my part nonetheless. I'm so proud of them, and so amazed at who they are becoming.

When I looked back on the first moments of fatherhood, I was comforted by the thought that I was concerned at the beginning. I realized that it was something powerful and comforting, with the fact that I was so deeply concerned about becoming a loving, supportive, present, and intentional father. It shows just how deeply prepared I already was. My worries, though discomforting, reflected my heart's deep desire to break the cycle of absence, hurt, and uncertainty that I experienced.

It is important for you to hear this clearly now: Your father's absence has no reflection on who you're going to be as a parent. Childhood wounds do not predetermine your future relationships with your children. You are not bound by a curse to repeat history. Instead, your experiences have uniquely equipped you to become an intentional, compassionate, and loving father. You've seen firsthand the cost of absence in a child's life and the emotional neglect that comes with it, and so it is shaping your heart to deeply value presence, love, and connection.

As you know, I've never really been one to sugarcoat things, and this letter is no different; So, I'm not going to sugarcoat the fact that navigating parenthood without a healthy parental model will come with its own set of challenges. There will be times when you question your instincts or second-guess the decisions you've made. There will certainly be plenty of times when you will feel inadequate, especially when clear guidance would have been helpful. There may be nights spent awake, asking yourself how to handle certain situations or worries about whether you're doing enough. A tip for you on this journey: If you make a mistake, teach those children about humility. Teach them about what a *real* apology looks like, and move forward.

I've said it several times so far, and I'll say it again: If you walk with Jesus, you're **never** alone. This applies even in fatherhood. Though you didn't have the earthly father you deserved in your childhood, you will always have a Heavenly Father who lovingly and intentionally guides you each step of the way. Psalm 32:8 beautifully assures us of God's constant presence and guidance: *"I will instruct you and teach you the way you should go; I will counsel you with My eye upon you."* He walks with you daily, offering wisdom, comfort, and assurance in who you are.

Beyond that, remember that God has graciously placed other supportive figures into your life as well—mentors, friends, parents of friends, and spiritual leaders who model healthy parenting in their own unique ways. Look to them. Lean into the lessons they can teach you, their wisdom, their experiences, and their genuine love and care for you. Allow them to speak truth and encouragement into your journey. It's not a weakness to ask for support—it's wisdom, humility, and strength. It displays all three of these when you can admit when you cannot do it on your own and need some help.

One thing you will quickly learn as a parent is that perfection is neither achievable nor necessary. Parenthood isn't about always having an answer or getting things right. It's about presence, intentionality, grace, and love. It's about showing up consistently, loving deeply, and being willing to admit when you were wrong or uncertain. Parenting without a model will teach you vulnerability, openness, humility, and reliance upon God— qualities that strengthen your relationship with your children in ways you may not yet fully understand. You will discover the incredible freedom of creating your own path—shaped by your experiences, guided by your values, and strengthened by your faith. You're not bound by expectations or limited by the past; instead, you have the beautiful opportunity to intentionally create the kind of family environment you always wished you'd had.

Your journey will teach you all of these lessons I've shared with you along this path of discovering Our Father's Love. Profound lessons about yourself, about God, and about unconditional love. Your children will not require perfection from you—they will only desire your genuine presence, love, and care. And that, dear younger me, you are absolutely equipped to provide in abundance.

The days will come when old fears resurface, but in those moments, do not despair. Breathe deeply, and remember that you are uniquely prepared for the sacred role and vocation of married life and parenthood—not in spite of your past, but because of it. Your journey through fatherlessness has given you insight, empathy, and strength to love more deeply, intentionally, and purposefully. As you step forward, trust in God's presence. Trust your heart. Trust your capacity to love. And trust in the beautiful, redemptive story God is writing through you and your future family.

With heartfelt compassion, deep understanding, and unwavering belief in your ability to parent beautifully,
Your Older Self

When we come across points in our lives that require us to face the unknown, it can be daunting. Entering parenthood without having experienced the consistent presence of a father can feel like stepping into unknown territory without a map. I know that's how it felt for me. When I held my daughter for the first time in that hospital room, joy and excitement filled my heart—but with that joy came quiet and persistent fear. I wondered how I would learn how to be a good father when I lacked a tangible example from my own childhood.

If you're feeling the same way, please hear me clearly: you are not alone. Parenthood under "normal" circumstances is difficult, let alone not having a model of "proper parenthood." There is no one correct way to parent. Parenthood is both rewarding and challenging, and the uncertainties that come with parenting without a healthy model can magnify these emotions. But your past experiences, no matter how challenging, do not have the power to dictate or predestine the type of parent you become.

In this chapter, I will share honestly what I learned from navigating parenthood without a clear example, and how you, too, can build a loving, nurturing environment for your children—even if you didn't have one yourself.

As I became a father, it forced me to confront the deepest fears rooted in my father's absence. Several questions echoed in my heart: "Will I make the same mistakes?" "How can I be sure I won't repeat harmful patterns?" "Can I truly provide emotional security when I've lacked it myself?" To address these fears, you first need to understand them. These are not fears of weakness; rather, they demonstrate your genuine desire to do better and provide something more meaningful for your children. Recognizing these fears is the first step toward addressing them honestly and compassionately.

The toughest part of navigating parenthood without a healthy example is the fear of repeating the same negative cycles. That is the real challenge. Without intentional awareness, we might unconsciously replicate these harmful behaviors. The realization is not meant to scare you—it's meant to empower you. Knowledge is power, and knowing that a harmful cycle is present makes it easier to address it.

Understanding generational cycles helps you consciously choose a healthier path. For example, if you experienced emotional neglect, you can intentionally choose to be emotionally attentive and available to your children. If abandonment characterized your childhood, you can purposefully commit yourself to consistent presence in your child's life. Romans 12:2 offers powerful encouragement: *"Do not be conformed to this world, but be transformed by the renewal of your mind, that you may prove what is the will of God, what is good and acceptable and perfect."* Your commitment to breaking harmful patterns is evidence of God's transformative work already happening within you.

You need to be willing to accept the gift of imperfection. For those of us who grew up without healthy parental models, perfectionism often creeps into our parenting as an attempt to compensate for our own childhood deficiencies. Initially, I placed enormous pressure on myself to always say the right things, make perfect choices, and never let my children down. But that mindset quickly proved unsustainable and unhealthy.

A freeing lesson that I experienced is when I learned that accepting imperfection meant that I was a good father. What my children needed wasn't perfection—it was consistent love, authenticity, and a willingness to learn from my mistakes. Incidentally, these are also the lessons that I would like my children to witness me learn because they will be able to see it in action and implement it in their own lives as they get older. It forms a healthy foundation in their life.

So, you may be asking, what is a healthy foundation? Well, moments in your daily lives with your children using the above concepts are a great start. These intentional choices will form a healthy foundation over time that offers your child security, stability, and emotional nourishment.

Additionally, it will help to clearly identify your values

- **Presence** — Actively choose to show up in your child's daily life, even in small moments

- **Emotional Openness** — Create a home where emotions are shared openly, safely, and authentically

- **Healthy Boundaries** — Set appropriate boundaries that encourage respect, responsibility, and security

- **Spiritual Guidance** — Introduce your children to God's love early through your example and by having intentional conversations about faith

Just because you are navigating parenthood without a healthy model doesn't mean that you have to do it alone. As they say, "it takes a village." God graciously places people in our lives who serve as valuable resources and guides. Take advantage of them. You cannot be introverted and expect to build a support network. This is an example of where our discussion on vulnerability comes into play. Proverbs 15:22 wisely advises: *"Without counsel plans go wrong, but with many advisers they succeed."* Seek wisdom proactively, knowing that God provides generously through others if you ask Him to. Consider the following on your path of seeking wisdom and guidance:

- **Find Mentors** — Seek experienced parents whom you respect. Observe their interactions and ask questions openly

- **Build Community** — Engage in parenting groups, church community, or other support networks. Community is essential in providing emotional support and practical wisdom

- **Professional Support** — Consider family counseling or parenting workshops. Professional insight can greatly strengthen your parenting skills

Despite how daunting it can be, your parenting journey can bring remarkable healing to your heart. I found profound emotional restoration in offering my children what I had missed—consistent love from a paternal source, a nurturing presence, and emotional security. In providing for their emotional and spiritual needs, God graciously healed parts of my heart I hadn't realized were still wounded.

Healing comes when we choose vulnerability over fear, openness over isolation, and authenticity over perfectionism. I've said it already, your children do not need you to have all the answers; they simply need you to walk with them openly and lovingly through life's uncertainties. Psalm 147:3 makes a beautiful promise: *"He heals the brokenhearted and binds up their wounds."* Allow parenting to become a healing ground for you—not only for your children but also for yourself.

My early faith formation was deeply distorted, and my view of God as a Father was skeptical. This was the result of growing up without a healthy earthly father relationship. Ironically, the most transformational part of my parenting journey was discovering God's perfect fatherhood for myself. It made complete sense too because after all, when we were created, we were created in His image. The demonstration of what healthy earthly fatherhood should look like is what God's Fatherhood looks like. That is what He based it off of.

And so, as I leaned into God's unwavering love, I learned what fatherhood truly means. God's love became my blueprint for parenting. His patience, compassion, steadfastness, and unconditional acceptance became qualities I actively sought to emulate. Embracing God's fatherhood redeemed and reshaped my understanding of parenting in the most powerful of ways. Romans 8:15 reassures: *"For you did not receive the spirit of slavery to fall back into fear, but you have received the spirit of sonship. When we cry, 'Abba! Father!'"* In understanding your own adoption as God's child, you will discover the foundation for your own role as a parent.

Moving forward in this process requires intentionality because that is what is required when navigating parenthood without a model. Here are some tangible steps you can implement today:

- **Pray for Guidance** — Regularly seek God's wisdom and discernment in parenting decisions

- **Reflect Regularly** — Identify area of parenting that trigger your anxiety or uncertainty. Address these proactively through prayer, study, support, and therapy

- **Educate Yourself** — Read parenting books, listen to podcasts, and attend workshops. Knowledge builds confidence. I heard a saying once that said: "You can't pray to God for a hole while leaning on a shovel." Your own investment and elbow grease is required, so get to work

- **Practice Intentional Presence** — Dedicate focused, distraction-free time daily with your children, showing consistent interest in their lives. **Put the cell phone down!** I'm telling you because I struggle too, and it will become a problem in the future when your children can only remember seeing the top of your head

- **Create Family Traditions** — Establish routine and tradition within your household. This will create wonderful memories, stability, predictability, and security to your children

Your parenting journey, despite beginning without a clear model, can become one of immense beauty, redemption, and grace. You're not merely surviving parenthood; you're redefining it through intentionality, love, and faith. Trust that God is fully capable and deeply committed to walking with you through every challenge you will face, every question you will ask, and every uncertainty you will experience. He is the perfect Father, and through Him, your journey in parenthood will become a story of restoration, healing, and generational blessing. Remember always: your past does not write your story or represent you, and it does not limit or predestine you to the kind of parent that you will become. Your intentional choices today will shape your entire branch of the family tree, and it will leave behind you a legacy of love and presence in the minds and hearts of your children, your grandchildren, and your grandchildren's children, going on forever until we are all reunited again in Our Father's Love. You are more equipped, more loved, and more capable than you've ever imagined. Trust the journey to come, it is beautiful.

Resources for Further Support

If you're navigating parenthood without a healthy model, these resources can offer vital support:

Professional Counseling & Support

- Focus on the Family Counseling

- BetterHelp Online Counseling

- Psychology Today Therapist Directory

Books for Further Reading

- *Parenting from the Inside Out* by Daniel Siegel and Mary Hartzell

- *The Connected Parent* by Karyn Purvis and Lisa Qualls

- *Shepherding a Child's Heart* by Tedd Tripp

Podcasts & Websites

- Risen Motherhood Podcast

- Dad Tired

- The Allender Center

Chapter 14

WHEN DEATH CREATES THE VOID

Dear Friend,

There are few, or dare I say no, pains in this world more profound than death. It is a somber reminder that there will come an end to our lives and the lives of those we love most deeply, and yes, this includes our animals as well. If you have experienced the loss of your father through death, I am so sorry for your loss. I cannot imagine how you feel. For many years, I feared that I, too, would experience this before having the opportunity to reconnect and reconcile with my father. You have my deepest condolences as the loss of a father hits your heart in such a painful way.

Perhaps your loss occurred suddenly, leaving you stunned and numb. Or perhaps it unfolded slowly, allowing you time to process and prepare, but with the added cost of being unable to ease the pending ache you knew was coming. Either way, the moment your father passed away, your life irrevocably changed, and your heart began navigating a deeply personal grief—one for which no one is ever fully prepared to experience.

While I have not personally experienced this loss, I believe I can empathize with you because I have lost my mother. Growing up without my dad, my mother took on the roles of both mom and dad. She needed to, whether she wanted to or not. Then, in October 2022, my mother succumbed to organ failure and passed away. I can tell you that I, too, felt lost and numb when she died.

Right now, your emotions must feel like they are impossible to unravel. I know mine were when I went to the hospital that night to say my good-byes. You grieve not only the man your father was; you're also grieving the wonderful memories you created and the countless moments, milestones, or experiences you anticipated sharing with him. Or, if you're like me, you may be grieving the loss of what could have been. The dreams that you wanted to experience with him by your side.

I wish I could sit with you right now, and in a way, I am. As your eyes skim these words, know I stand with you, just like Jesus. As the grief continues to unravel, you will be reminded that it is both immediate and long-term simultaneously. You grieve the advice he can no longer impart to you, the events he can no longer attend, the encouragement you need, and those quiet conversations that will never happen. It is difficult, and grief is subjective. Everyone is different, and they all grieve differently. Allow yourself that grace. Feel this grief the way you need to feel it. Process it the way you need to process it. It will only bottle up inside if you don't let it out the way you need to.

I wanted to share some thoughts that might encourage healing during this difficult time. Your heartache is valid, and it deserves recognition and space. Regardless of your father-child relationship and what it looked like in your situation. No one can measure your grief by how long you had your father or how deeply you felt connected to him. The simple truth is that the absence he leaves behind is real, and it is life-changing. It is a void no one else can fill—it is a space that is uniquely his.

As heavy as this weight pulls on your heart, I wanted to offer something deeply important: a hope that is gentle and powerful. While your father's presence here has come to an end, there is a Father whose presence never ends, remaining constant, steadfast, and faithful—the same Father who created *your* father. Your Heavenly Father sees your pain intimately, He holds each tear you shed, and walks closely beside you in this valley of grief. His compassion runs deeper than any earthly love you've experienced, and His strength can sustain you even in your most fragile moments.

Psalm 34:18 promises us: "The Lord is near to the brokenhearted and saves the crushed in spirit." Right now, more than ever, I urge you to lean into this truth. Invite God into your heart, mind, and soul. Invite Him into the places that your earthly father's absence left vacant. Allow Him to lovingly provide the comfort, guidance, and peace your heart desperately needs. God will never erase the love you have for the father you lost; He is the one who placed him in your life to begin with, so that wouldn't make any sense. God will just gently step into your grief, bearing its pain with you, with compassion, grace, and unwavering tenderness. He will offer to be your Father in the deepest, most meaningful sense of the word. Only He is able to do this, because He is the one who invented fatherhood.

In the pages ahead, my hope is that you will find the comfort in knowing that your grief is understood, your pain recognized, and your longing validated. Even more importantly, I pray for you that you will discover a closeness with God that sustains, heals, and transforms your life. The passing of your father out of this life and into the next has undeniably left a permanent mark on your story, but death is not the final word. Within this loss, God is already present. He is ready to guide your heart toward healing. He is hoping that you will ask for His intercession and for a deeper understanding of His fatherly love.

With heartfelt compassion and earnest prayers,
Your friend on this journey

Losing a father is a life-altering experience—one that no one can truly prepare for. It marks the beginning of a journey you never asked to take, yet you must somehow navigate. Your world shifted the moment he passed from this earth, regardless of whether it was sudden or expected. The path ahead looks vastly different, and each step feels unsure and disorienting. This new journey will often leave you to ask yourself: "Who am I without him?" Recall the chapter you've read on our identities. Our identity is in the One who created us: God. Yet, you may still feel like your identity has partly been stripped from you when your father passed away, and that's okay. After all, he was your earthly father and is fifty percent of who you now are.

A father's role is unique. He is to offer guidance, stability, protection, and a lasting identity, even when he will ultimately have to leave you behind as he continues his journey with our Lord Jesus. I am not blind to the fact that losing him can feel like losing a vital reference point in your life. It's not simply losing a loved one; you are losing part of the map you once used to navigate life. Suddenly, the milestones you looked forward to have become fantasies in moments of quiet reflection, reminders of what could have been.

While this loss is deeply significant, it does not mean that your journey forward is without direction or purpose. Your Heavenly Father awaits you, intimately present and standing ready to provide clarity on the road ahead. If you humbly ask Him, He gladly and freely provides wisdom when this life seems impossible to navigate. Although your earthly father's influence is no longer tangible, his impact on you remains.

I feel that the hardest part of grief is the fact that you are required to face reality. You have to confront the idea that your father is no longer physically present on this earth. When I lost my mom, this was the hardest pill to swallow. It took over a year to stop instinctively reaching for my phone to call her. There is a process of grief in our lives that is commonly taught among medical professionals. The acronym DABDA is the guide, and it stands for denial, anger, bargaining, depression, and acceptance. While each person is different and may move forward or backward along this path or even skip one, most will hit each mark at some point along their grief journey.

Along this path, just know that you may find yourself expressing some unexpected emotions. You may feel moments of heated anger for your father leaving too soon, or anger directed at God for taking him from you. You may feel deep regret at things that were left unsaid or actions for which you didn't have a chance to reconcile. These feelings are valid and are natural aspects of grieving. It is essential to allow yourself to feel them as they come and usher them back out. You don't want to harbor them too long and bottle them up, which may make you feel worse. It is important that you allow yourself the freedom to experience these emotions without judgment. Acknowledging your grief is the first step toward healing: a meaningful healing, not one that leaves behind scar tissue. Allowing yourself to grieve authentically in the ways you need to experience grief will open the door for genuine restoration and growth.

In the absence created by death, you can experience God's fatherhood in new ways. You've been blessed by God to have your earthly father with you until now, but his mission is complete, and the tasks assigned to him are finished, so God called him home. Now, you are called on to cultivate deeper ties to God as your Father. He doesn't offer consolation from afar. He steps intimately into the grief you are experiencing.

The story of Jesus raising Lazarus from the dead comes to mind. Known as the shortest verse in the Bible, it says in John 11:35, "Jesus wept." This was when the sisters of Lazarus, Mary and Martha, ran to Jesus, saying that if He had been present, Lazarus would not have died. Jesus wept with them because of how much He loved Lazarus and how sad He was at his death. However, Jesus used Lazarus' death for a higher purpose. Jesus raised Lazarus from the dead to prove who He was. Just so, will He step into our grief if we allow Him to, becoming the Father who provides wisdom, compassion, and presence in the deepest moments of sorrow.

Scripture provides clarity on God's role as Father. Romans 8:15 reminds us: "For you did not receive the spirit of slavery to fall back into fear, but you have received the spirit of sonship. When we cry, "Abba! Father!" it is the Spirit Himself bearing witness with our spirit that we are children of God." This relationship with God offers comfort, unlike any earthly relationship. Remember, God's definition of fatherhood is what we live by. He is the first Father, and in His fatherhood, there is unchanging stability, perfect guidance, and unwavering love. Allow God's fatherly care to become more than an abstract belief in your life—let it become reality.

As we experience loss, we find it challenging to trust in God. We often hear someone say, "Why did He allow this?" This question often becomes a barrier. However, it can also become an entry point into deeper, more honest dialogue. Several ask this question and withdraw from Him, which is the exact opposite you should do. His reasons will always make sense, maybe not in the here and now, but later, once we are on God's side of eternity. We need to be willing to use this opportunity to approach God honestly and vulnerably. He welcomes your questions, anger, sorrow, and doubts. He is strong enough to handle them.

Consider the example of King David in the Psalms, who often voiced confusion, doubt, and frustration toward God. God didn't grow angry at this, and He didn't condemn David for this. Instead, through his honest expression, David's relationship with God deepened. Psalm 13:1-2 demonstrates this: "How long, O Lord? Wilt thou forget me forever? How long wilt thou hide thy face from me? How long must I bear pain in my soul, and have sorrow in my heart all the day?" Expressing your true feelings to God isn't disrespectful or faithless; it's the path toward deeper intimacy and healing. Your honesty invites Him into the most wounded parts of your heart, where He can bring the most meaningful healing.

After my mom passed away, I felt I had tunnel vision. I was in shock. Grief has a way of doing this, of narrowing our vision. It makes you feel isolated. Yet, in that isolation, God promises His presence in the middle of the pain. Deuteronomy 31:8 is a powerful reminder: "It is the Lord who goes before you; He will be with you; He will not fail you or forsake you; do not fear or be dismayed." God is present with you in these difficult times. He continuously offers His ever-abiding presence to sustain you. Seek tangible ways to experience His closeness—through prayer, worship, scripture, and community. You will discover Him near in moments of quiet reflection, in comfort offered by others, and even in simple moments of unexpected peace.

I understand that an undeniable emptiness has been left behind in your father's absence. I remember feeling that emptiness, too. I fought hard to find ways to fill that emptiness, and spoiler alert, I never was successful until I leaned on God for help. One way to cope with his absence is to preserve and honor his legacy meaningfully. Reflect on the virtues he embodied and held close to his heart. What were the lessons, character traits, and values that he demonstrated? Allow them to guide and inspire your decisions. Ask yourself: "What would Dad do?"

Consider incorporating his memory into your future endeavors. Maybe he valued compassion, hard work, integrity, or kindness. Embracing these values in your own life will honor him and ensure that his influence continues to positively impact the world through you. We often hear the metaphor that our actions have ripple effects, like a pebble dropped in water. Implementing your father's influence in your life to carry it forward is the ripple effect of his actions while he was still here on earth. If your relationship with your father had complications, that's okay. Use this moment to reflect on areas you wish you had been different. Allow these reflections to inspire growth and change so you can create a healthier, hopeful legacy for your own life.

As you begin to build a new normal for yourself, know that God is with you. The process isn't easy, and it will require courage, patience, and intentionality. As you make progress moving forward, you will find yourself establishing new traditions, rhythms, and relationships that reflect your growth and healing. Invite God into this process. Seek His wisdom through each step, and allow Him to be your anchor. This is especially true as you build new routines and relationships that reflect your deepest values. Embracing God's guidance will help you to navigate this new life without the direct influence of your dad. Allowing God to be who He is, your Heavenly Father, will provide comfort and purpose.

Your grief, while painful, gives you perspective. It will allow you to comfort and encourage others experiencing similar losses. As your healing journey progresses, your story will slowly become a source of empathy and compassion. It will enable you to comfort those who share your pain, and be a tool for God to use as He blesses others through you. 2 Corinthians 1:3-4 is a perfect reflection: "Blessed be the God and Father of our Lord Jesus Christ...who comforts us in all our affliction, so that we may be able to comfort those who are in any affliction." Your journey carries power, and when shared with those sharing your pain, it can transform sorrow into ministry and bring healing and comfort to those around you.

While your father's death created a permanent shift in your life, it is not the end of your story. God promises to walk with you through this pain, offering steadfast love, comfort, and presence as you walk through each new day in your healing journey. You feel this grief deeply and painfully, but it is not without hope or purpose. Let God guide you forward, transforming your loss into strength, empathy, compassion, and deeper faith. Your Heavenly Father's love and care will sustain you, helping you to build a future that honors your earthly father's legacy and embraces the profound hope that God offers us at each sunrise and each new step of our journey.

Reflection & Application

Reflection Questions

1. How can embracing God's fatherhood transform your grief into a deeper relationship with Him?

2. What qualities or lessons from your father's life can you intentionally embody to honor his legacy?

3. How might your grief uniquely equip you to minister compassionately to others?

Devotional Thought

"The steadfast love of the Lord never ceases, his mercies never come to an end; they are new every morning." – Lamentations 3:22-23 (RSV-2CE)

Recommended Reading

- *Grieving with Hope* by Samuel J. Hodges IV & Kathy Leonard

- *A Grace Disguised* by Jerry Sittser

Recommended Songs

- "Homesick" by MercyMe

- "Praise You in This Storm" by Casting Crowns

- "Even If" by MercyMe

Chapter 15

MY FINAL ENCOURAGEMENT FOR YOU ON YOUR JOURNEY

D EAR Reader,
I promised I would check back in with you at the end! I'm glad you made it, and I'm so proud of you and the journey we just shared together. I hope you got something out of it and learned a few things along the way. As we come to the end of this journey together, I wanted to take a moment to speak directly to you. I hope the words you've read within these pages have offered you comfort, insight, and hope. I know that life can be filled with challenges, doubts, and questions, especially when you've grown up without the guidance of a father. I want to remind you that your story is not yet finished, and the pages ahead hold incredible promise and value. So, don't give up the fight!

Throughout this book, we've explored many themes that have shaped my journey, and I hope they resonate with you as well. We began by confronting the void left by an absent father and acknowledging the pain and questions that came with it. I shared my first encounter with faith, that pivotal moment when I realized I wasn't alone—that a loving Heavenly Father was watching over me, ready to fill the gaps in my heart.

We delved into the search for identity, learning that our true worth and identity are found not in the world's ever-changing standards, but in the unchanging love of God. Embracing God as our Father means trusting in His promises, knowing that His plans for us are good, even when we can't see the path ahead. We discussed the importance of building a strong relationship with God, realizing that it's a journey of daily connection, trust, and perseverance. Through this relationship, we find the strength to navigate the ups and downs of life, knowing that God is with us every step of the way.

Forgiveness and healing were key themes as well. Facing painful truths is never easy, but it's necessary for true freedom. Letting go of anger and bitterness allows us to experience the overwhelming power of God's love and grace, transforming our hearts and opening us up to a life filled with peace and joy.

We also explored the role of father figures, recognizing that God often places people in our lives to guide and encourage us. These figures can reflect His love and wisdom, helping us grow and learn, even in the absence of a biological father.

Finding purpose and direction is a journey that begins when we trust God and step out in faith. Your purpose is not to achieve perfection, but to live authentically and use your talents to make a difference in the world. Remember that every experience and challenge is preparing you for something greater. Embracing your story means accepting every aspect of your journey—both the successes and the setbacks—as part of who you are. Your story is a testament to God's faithfulness, a reflection of His work in your life, and a source of encouragement to those around you.

Navigating parenthood without a model may seem daunting, but you are equipped with everything you need. Lean on God's guidance, surround yourself with a supportive community, and trust that you are capable of being the parent your child needs.

As you continue your journey, I want to offer a few final words of encouragement:

1. **Trust in God's Love**: No matter what you've been through, God's love for you is so much greater, and it is unchanging and eternal. You are His beloved child, and He is always with you, guiding you and holding you close. Just be held.

2. **Embrace Your Story**: Every part of your journey matters. Let go of the shame and fear of what others will think about your experiences and allow God to use your story to bring hope and healing to others. Just like He did by leading me to write this book.

3. **Seek God's Presence:** Make time for God in your daily life. Pray, read His Word, and listen for His voice. He is the source of your strength and the anchor in every storm.

4. **Live Authentically:** Be true to who God created you to be. Use your gifts, passions, and experiences to make a difference in the world, knowing that your life has a unique purpose.

5. **Extend Grace:** Offer grace to yourself and others. We all make mistakes, but God's grace is sufficient for every moment. Let love and forgiveness guide your relationships.

6. **Stay Connected:** Surround yourself with a community that supports and encourages you in your walk of faith. We are stronger together, and God often uses others to speak His truth into our lives.

7. **Be Patient:** You'll recall that over the course of this book, I've repeated the idea that everything is a journey, and that's because it is. None of what you've read within these pages happened magically or overnight. By presenting our prayers and petitions to God, we need to be patient to hear His response. Everything comes at its proper time. In today's day and age, we've become accustomed to instant gratification. You cannot expect that to happen here. This book is my story over the course of *30 years*. So, be patient; it is a virtue. God will move when it's time. Trust Him and trust His timing. I know it seems daunting. 30 years seems crazy to think about until you're standing there. At the end of the day, remember that you are called by name and belong to Him. As such, time is irrelevant. Eventually, you'll be experiencing eternal life anyway, and 30 years will seem like a second.

As you close this book and step back into your own story, know that you are not alone. There are others out there who have felt the pain you're feeling, myself included. God is with you. He is cheering you on, running with you, and matching you step for step. I recall the poem "Footprints," when it talks about walking along a beach with the Lord and looking back to only see one set of footprints at the most difficult points of life. It was then that the Lord was carrying you through the hardest points of life. Never forget this metaphor because God will *never* forsake us.

Your journey is a beautiful tapestry being woven by His loving hands, and I am so grateful to have shared part of it with you. I am so humbled and honored that your eyes have skimmed these pages, because everything I've written here has just been proven true. Everything I went through led to a greater purpose for my life, just as it will for you.

And so, I thank you for being part of my tapestry as well. May God bless you abundantly, filling your life with His love, peace, comfort, and joy as you continue to seek Him and embrace the incredible story that He is writing for you. Be receptive, be open-minded, because you have absolutely no idea what He could have in store for you. Isn't that exciting?

Epilogue

THE wipers swayed rhythmically, brushing aside steady streams of April rain. I sat quietly in the back seat of my mother's purple Chrysler PT Cruiser; my eyes fixated on the droplets hitting the windshield while the trees whizzed by. Each drop blurred the gray sky outside, mirroring the swirl of emotions within my chest. My older half-brother Joshua sat silently in the passenger seat, one hand in his lap and the other casually resting on the windowsill as he watched out the window. I watched the back of his head, wondering if he felt as nervous as I did. After all, he got to experience what my dad was like in the early years while I was too young to remember.

Mom navigated the car carefully along the back roads toward the rural cemetery, eventually pulling onto the shoulder, gravel softly crunching beneath the tires. I looked out the window to see a gently sloping hill, capped with a tombstone bearing my last name in large block lettering: "HOLBROOK." The silence inside the car felt heavy, almost palpable. As we paused, taking in the reality of what was about to happen, we noticed the group gathered at the top of the hill, just past its crest and beyond the tombstone marking the occasion. As I began to brace myself for the day's upcoming events, my mind was flooded with details and stories about how I got to this moment.

* * *

It was another one of those ordinary days that seemed unremarkable until it wasn't. I heard the booming voice of my stepfather, Bill, calling for my mom to join him in the basement. His tone of voice was attention-grabbing. It was gentle, yet tense—a quiet seriousness, followed by careful hesitation. It made me pause as I quietly leaned closer to the basement door. I could slightly make out what they were whispering. "What's going on?" Mom asked, her voice cautious and uncertain. Bill cleared his throat. "I found something you need to see," he said. The unmistakable clicks of the mouse and keyboard were followed by silence and then a sharp intake of breath from Mom. "His grandfather," he said, "He passed away last week."

Mom sighed softly, "How did you find this?" "I was surfing the internet and recognized the name," he said. "There's something else. The obituary says that the funeral already happened, but the burial is scheduled for later this week." There was another pause, likely Mom trying to process the information she received and the emotions that came with it. "Do you think he'll be there?" Bill said, his voice quiet. "Volley?" she confirmed softly. "Yes, I do. He wouldn't miss it."

As I sat quietly on the top step, eavesdropping on the conversation, I stiffened at her comment. I'd imagined the moment of meeting my dad several times. Often, it was filled with anger and hatred. I pictured myself yelling and screaming at him, even hitting him, demanding that he tell me why he chose his vices over me, why he wasn't strong enough to overcome them for my sake. Other times, it was soft, almost therapeutic. It was likely my heart's attempt to make peace with the situation and move forward in the gentlest way possible. And now, suddenly, it felt both terrifying and within reach.

"Should we tell him?" she asked. "Is it fair to ask him to make that choice?" Bill hesitated a moment before responding carefully. "He's old enough to understand. I think he deserves to have the option." I stared at my feet resting on the top step when my mom called for Joshua. He wasn't far away, so his response revealed my presence. He went downstairs and was filled in on the situation, at which point he was asked if he would go on the trip with us if we decided to go, and he agreed. "Brenton," she called gently, knowingly, "come here, please," I responded to her request, quickly scaling the stairs, but my face was still flushed from the embarrassment of being discovered.

She stooped down to my level and confirmed, "You heard?" I nodded slowly, glancing at Bill for a moment. "We just learned that your grandfather passed away," Mom said softly, reaching out to take my hands into hers. "I'm so sorry you didn't get the chance to meet him. He was kind, and so was your grandmother. I'll never forget how they treated me. They were sweet, and it was wonderful to know them." I nodded again, not knowing how to express the strange ache I felt at their loss despite never meeting them. "But," she continued, "if we go to your grandfather's burial, it's likely your dad will be there." She watched my expressions carefully and closely.

As these words hung in the air, I felt excitement at the opportunity to close a chapter of my life that had haunted me for so long. "We won't make you do anything you don't want to do," she said, "you get to decide if you're ready to meet him." "I'm ready," I said, with minimal hesitation. "Are you sure? You don't have to decide now." "I'm sure," I replied. "I will make arrangements then," she said. "Can we bring some flowers for grandpa and grandma?" "Absolutely."

As everybody returned to what they were doing, no doubt with an inexplicable shock in their minds, I took a deep breath. I felt both relieved and uncertain. The weight of the choice that I just made was hitting me, and I contemplated changing my mind several times. I leaned against the basement wall, and in the dimness surrounding me, I knew that whatever I decided would change my life forever. As always, my mother's words comforted me when this topic arose. I knew I was supported, no matter what, and that reassurance was all I needed.

I turned toward the staircase, ready to ascend once more, but this time, I carried the real possibility that I would meet the man who had caused so much pain and sadness. But in that quiet, decisive moment, I felt a strange feeling of comfort, seemingly out of nowhere, showered upon me. At that moment, I realized that a metaphorical intermission in the theatrical production of my life was about to end. The story's climax was almost over, and the unexpected possibility of meeting the father I had never known was the quiet and powerful hope of the second act. It symbolized that my story was continuing on the path it was meant to.

* * *

Today wasn't just a day to say goodbye to a grandfather and grandmother I never knew—it was the day that I would finally meet my dad for the first time. Almost eleven years of waiting, wondering, hoping, and fearing came to this moment amid the damp grass, solemn gravestones, and a cold spring drizzle. Mom took a deep breath and looked at Joshua and me before saying, "Let me make sure that he is here and that he is okay." She steadied herself before stepping out into the misty rain. She glanced toward the top of the hill, her eyes scanning carefully, and as she crested the hill, she disappeared into the crowd at the top.

Joshua and I waited quietly in the car, watching her ascend the hill with careful steps. The rain continued, softly tapping against the car's roof, matching the restless drumming of my fingers against the armrest. A short moment passed, and then the crowd began moving toward us. Expecting it to stop at the gravestone bearing my last name, I was surprised when the majority walked to the bottom of the hill, meeting the car where it was parked along that busy state route.

From the car window, I watched my mother approach with the crowd in tow and let Joshua out of the front seat, leaving the door cracked open. He approached a man silhouetted against the backdrop of the gray, rain-soaked countryside, shook his hand, and embraced him briefly. They shared a few words, and I watched the crowd begin to turn toward the grave site as Mom looked at me through the tinted window. "Volley," she said loudly. The same man that Joshua had briefly embraced turned his head toward her. "Your son is here. He wants to place flowers at his grandparents' grave," she said. I heard the audible gasp from several people in the crowd. She opened my door, and I stepped out, prepared to shake his hand as she had told me to. As I put my hand out, he grabbed it, quickly pulling me into a tight hug.

I heard quiet whimpers from several people in the crowd, whom I'd later learn were my aunts and their families. It felt nice to be with him finally. To experience the hug I had so desperately wanted for so long. He pulled away, and we made eye contact. "Hi," he said, breaking the sounds of the crowd, his voice quieter and softer than I had anticipated. He hesitated momentarily, probably trying to process something as unexpected as reuniting with me on what otherwise would be such a sad day. "I'm glad you're here," he said. "Me too," I replied.

"I brought flowers—wreaths—for grandpa and grandma," I said. His expression softened to a gentle mixture of sadness and gratitude. "Thank you. They would love them." We took the wreaths from the trunk, slowly walking them to the gravestone and gently placing them prominently on each side. The colors on the wreaths, bright and hopeful, provided a brief contrast to the somberness of the gathering clouds. For a moment, we stood in silence, looking down at the resting place of my father's parents —the people whose lives shaped his—and, by extension, mine.

"I know this isn't how you probably imagined this would happen," he said slowly, his voice heavy with emotion. "Meeting like this—at a grave site. I'm sorry it happened this way." I paused, absorbing his words and noticing their sincerity. "It's okay," I finally whispered. "At least it's happening." His eyes glistened softly, and he nodded in agreement as though recognizing that this imperfect encounter offered a hopeful possibility for something better in a fragile situation.

The cars continued passing below on the state route nearby, their noise blending into the background. Dad took his coat off, placed it on me, and motioned at the minister to begin. His arm never left my shoulder for the entire service. The gentle rain continued falling, steady but soft, enveloping our private conversation. Mom and Joshua watched from a respectful distance, allowing us space to process this first encounter on our terms.

"I've thought a lot about this moment," he admitted quietly, still staring at the freshly dug hole in the earth that would soon hold my grandfather's cremated remains. "About what I'd say to you if I ever got the chance." I listened, my heart softening a little more with each word. This wasn't the angry confrontation I'd once imagined, nor was it the overwhelming reunion I'd quietly hoped for. It was simple and honest. And somehow, the serene setting of an April spring rain made it deeply meaningful in its natural peace.

"There's more that I can't change than what I can," he continued. But I want to do better if you'll let me." I saw the vulnerability on his face, etched with lines that told a story of struggle and regret. Standing there, beneath the quiet rain, I decided to give him that chance and let this imperfect meeting become something new.

We lingered longer together, quietly honoring my grandparents, who undoubtedly had a spiritual hand in this reunion. My father stood beside me, close enough now that I could feel his quiet presence—still uncertain, careful, but undeniably real. Eventually, we began to walk back down the hill toward the purple PT Cruiser parked on that gravel shoulder, the rain lifting briefly, a gentle reminder of the complex beauty of life's imperfect moments. My mother and Joshua moved toward us slowly, with careful smiles. This day, I realized, wasn't meant to resolve everything. But perhaps that wasn't the point. Maybe this meeting atop this hill was meant to begin something—to plant the seeds of understanding and compassion, watered gently by the quiet rains of April.

Joshua, Mom, and I got back into the PT Cruiser, leaving newly minted memories and those beautiful wreaths behind. We headed toward a rental hall reserved for the luncheon celebrating Grandpa's life—a luncheon where I would have a chance to ask some deeper questions, and have them answered by my dad. As we drove away, I looked back at the hill, representing the turning point of everything I had learned. "Thank you, Grandpa and Grandma," I whispered, "and thank God for me for answering my prayers."

ABOUT THE AUTHOR

Brenton Holbrook is a devoted follower of Jesus Christ, passionate about sharing the same message of hope, healing, and redemption laid on his heart by the Lord. Raised until aged 11, without his earthly father present, Brenton embarked on a personal journey to find meaning and purpose. While filled with deep, emotional pain, the path ahead ultimately led to the discovery of God's profound love for all of us and His desire for us to have a personal relationship with His son, Jesus. It is a love that filled the deepest chasms in Brenton's heart while still young. When he is not writing, Brenton works and has taught in higher education. He often volunteers with his local Veterans of Foreign Wars Post, of which he is a Life Member. He resides in Central Michigan with his family of 5, a dog named Onyx, and two cats, named Nermal and Princess.

www.ingramcontent.com/pod-product-compliance
Lightning Source LLC
Chambersburg PA
CBHW021151130626
46554CB00005B/1762